Discovering Your Inner Child

Transforming Toxic Patterns and Finding Your Joy

Asha Hawkesworth

Foreword by Ahnna Hawkesworth

Revised and Expanded Edition

Imaginalove Media

To my wife, Ahnna, who helped me understand myself,
and to my two children, Wren and Harry.
Together, all of you light up my life.

For additional inner child material and resources, visit:
www.brighthill.net

Third Edition, Revised and Expanded

www.imaginalovemedia.com

Book design by Asha Hawkesworth.

ISBN-13: 978-1542583114

ISBN-10: 154258311X

January 2017

Contents

Foreword

I believe that trust is innate in most human beings. It is also often the first thing compromised by careless cosmic footsteps, for many of us. I spent a lot of my early life feeling uncomfortable trusting other people, and I certainly didn't trust my own power. Conversely, when I did decide to trust, I often trusted those who were untrustworthy, which ultimately caused me to feel less trusting. It's one of those vicious cycles—a hamster wheel of unhappiness I didn't even know I was on.

I believe the trusting child waits in each one of us, sometimes burrowed quite deeply for protection. I think she cries sometimes or looks out on this great cosmic playground where it feels like only other people ever get to play. Our adult selves can be quite sternly directive about the way we expect the child inside of us to behave, but this child is our true nature. This child is our joy. No matter how hard we try to reason with her, she is always whining and cajoling for recognition. This child will play.

On the negative side, if we are acting unconsciously, our inner child can be the cause of destructive behaviors such as overspending, overeating, or drug addictions. She can willfully destroy relationships or even keep them from happening in the first place. She will pick playmates who repeat the patterns she knows, even though they make her miserable.

On the positive side, when we act consciously, our inner child can be a source of great light in our souls. When she is not bound by her anger or anything that happened to her in the past, she is the brush strokes on your canvas. She is the words on your page. She is the laughter that helps you to connect with others. She is the compassion that helps you feel gentle with yourself in an often painful world.

My own inner child cried in my heart for a long time. In the year before I met Asha, I did a lot of soul searching. I was restless and unhappy despite a good job, many very good friends, and a happy little nest I was glad to call home. But the deep truth, which only my Spirit knew, was that I felt unfulfilled. I felt like I was drifting hopelessly off course in a way I couldn't identify. I felt deeply sad. I knew that if I didn't pay attention, I would miss the place on the horizon where my greatest happiness lay. This does bear repeating: I knew that if I didn't pay attention, I would miss the place on the horizon where my greatest happiness lay.

I prayed so hard for answers about what I was supposed to do next that tears would stream down my cheeks. It took me awhile to realize that the answers had come fairly easily, but I didn't want to hear them. They were all terrifying. Here they are, in the order I heard them:

Move.
Lose the job.
Be open to what love looks like, or you will miss it.

In the course of that year, I moved to a bigger apartment in the building where I was living. Three days later, I discovered that my government job was slated for elimination. I certainly would not have moved if I had known this was going to happen. But because I moved, the woman who lived above my new apartment moved to my old apartment, and Asha moved in upstairs. This is not to say that I base my happiness on the existence of one other person on the planet, but she was the beacon on that point on the horizon where my greatest happiness lay, and she would tell you I was the same for her. We have had the great good fortune to embark on our journey of growth together, and it is because of this journey that this book was written.

Sometimes the most powerful thing you can do is trust where you are. Please read the words that follow and know that you are not alone in your journey. There is a way to love and joy despite anything that's happened to you. If you want to fight me and say that isn't so, I challenge you to listen to that voice in your soul that's been with you since childhood. This voice is the child you once were. Child is faith, and faith is the child in each one of us. Have faith in yourself that you can change the things you want to. There is a point on the horizon where your greatest happiness is. And there is every possibility you will find it.

Namaste.

Ahnna Hawkesworth
March 2011

Preface

When I was growing up, the story that my inner child learned about my family was one of perfection: we were the perfect family. My parents were perfect, our house was perfect and perfectly clean, our food was perfect, our health was perfect, and I, as the only child, also had to be perfect. Unfortunately, none of this was true. Even more unfortunately, however, my inner child believed that it *was* true, and I spent years trying to wear the mask of perfection and wondering why my feelings didn't seem to agree with the Family Myth.

As a child, I learned very quickly what was acceptable in a perfect household and what wasn't. "Negative" feelings were never acceptable. We were perfect, so there was no need to feel sad, angry, or depressed. Excessive joy, on the other hand, could be "too loud" and inappropriate, so that wasn't really acceptable, either. What was acceptable was the bland numbness of stuffing all of my feelings into a closet somewhere, leaving me ready to face the world with a placid mask that was designed to show everyone how calm, quiet, and simply perfect my life must be.

One of my earliest memories of our familial bliss was when my dad hit his head on a window and needed stitches. Back then, stitches were big, ugly, and black. He looked like Frankenstein with that big line of stitching across the middle of his forehead. He looked scary to me. He thought that was hilarious, so he purposely scared me multiple times. But of course, he was only kidding.

Most of the time, my dad wasn't kidding. He would explode in rage at the slightest provocation. I had no doubt that I had really screwed up something when it happened, but I never really knew what it was I had done. I tried very hard to avoid setting off the volcano, but the eruptions came anyway when I least expected them. I remember playing in the living room once, where he had fallen asleep. I wasn't being noisy, but something I did must have awakened him. He charged me from the couch, and my heart nearly stopped. I thought I was going to die right then. Fortunately, he never did anything. Dad wasn't physically violent like his mother was. He always told me how lucky I was not to have abusive parents like that. Of course, I agreed with him. We were a happy, normal family. This is what "normal" looked like.

When I was six years old, I played a game of "I'll show you mine if you show me yours" with a male cousin. We were curious. We were intrigued. My mother caught us, however, and I learned a big lesson that day: "good" people—perfect people—do not get naked with members of the opposite sex. My mother saw fit to call my aunt and uncle, my grandmother, and my father into the room so that I could be appropriately shamed before them all. And I was very ashamed. I learned that sexual feelings were not okay. Better hide those. I still couldn't help masturbating, but at least I managed to feel very guilty about it.

My tween years were difficult. Dad spent two years in Germany (he was in the army) while my mother and I stayed behind on the rural farmland they had bought to retire on. When Dad returned, it was obvious he wasn't sure if he wanted to stay married. No one was happy, and both of my parents became more embittered. But perfect people don't divorce, so they came to a sort of truce eventually. I was just trying to figure out what I could control in my life, which wasn't much. We lived three miles from a small town in Texas, and I couldn't drive. There were no kids close by. I was on my own.

I did develop the family sense of perfection at this time, however. My parents were always right, so whatever they thought was the right thing to think. Anyone who disagreed was "an idiot," as Dad would say. So by age 13, I felt pretty secure in my own superiority. I made better grades than the other kids and knew infinitely more than the teachers did. I didn't have many friends, though.

I was also fat during these years. It turns out that you can't be perfect and fat at the same time. I ate what was given me to eat, but it was still my fault that I was fat. "She has *such* a pretty face; it's just too bad she's so heavy." (These conversations always referred to me in the third person, even if I was standing right there.) Or my favorite, from my perfect mother, "Do you think if we put all three of them [my fat cousins and myself] in a bag, that any would fall out?"

I was schooled daily in how to be perfect. For a perfect kid in a perfect family, I sure heard a lot about my imperfections. I never could seem to do anything correctly. My mother, on the other hand, was the perfect housekeeper. All knick-knacks were kept under glass; otherwise, they might gather dust, which we were highly allergic to, she said. (It doesn't seem to bother me now.) Weekends were for cleaning, and clean I did. Many times. She made me vacuum the whole house three times in a row because I "missed some dirt." I never saw the dirt I missed, but she did. My inability to see the dirt must have been due to some imperfection in myself. There were a lot of those.

Perhaps to compensate for my imperfections at home, I was very perfect in school—annoyingly so. But some experiences in junior high made me humble. The principal gave me a heart-to-heart talk one day that really changed my attitude. It had never occurred to me that my arrogance was *hurtful.* In my heart, I didn't want to hurt anyone. I began to change after that. Over time, I became more accepting and open. Maybe I wasn't right *all the time.* Maybe no one was.

During these years, my mother found a new religion. She likes to be in control, and the near-debacle of a possible divorce probably pushed her over the edge. She didn't find God, though. In spite of being raised a Baptist, and retaining all of the "moral principles" of the Southern Baptist Church, she was never really interested in God. She never prayed. She never referred to God. Doing so would have taken attention away from her. Instead, she found a religion that could direct attention to her: nutrition.

After years of Shake 'n Bake, Lucky Charms, and Wonder bread, my mother decided that sugar and white flour were the Devil. Our bread had to be 100% whole wheat, our rice had to be brown, and a good dessert would never again darken our doorway—unless it was a Snickers bar. My mother loved Snickers bars. Those became an exception because they have high-fructose corn syrup in them instead of sugar. Somehow, that was okay. Oh, and except for pizza, too. Pizza may have a white crust, but it was... well, it was my mother's favorite food, so it was okay. Our vegetables did not have to be organic, though. Frozen vegetables, she maintained, are better for you than fresh vegetables, organic or not. There were a lot of rules, really, and they changed depending on which article she had read recently in *Prevention* magazine.

Dad and I adapted to this new religion as best we could, and it apparently wasn't all bad, because I did lose weight. By high school, I was slim and attractive again, at least according to my mother. Any compliment paid to me was as good as a compliment paid to her.

In high school, I became very good at conforming to my parents' mask. I studied hard. I had no social life, and few really close friends. I knew that dating wasn't really an option in my house; there was too much risk of physical contact that way—and that was the path to shame. I basically did whatever my parents wanted and dressed the way they thought I should dress. My mother always went shopping with me to pick my clothes.

As a perfectly smart child, I was expected to graduate Valedictorian of my class. I did not, and this failure could not belong to my family, so it was projected onto the school itself: it was rigged in favor of the Superintendent's child, my parents declared. Although I was initially upset by this "failure," I soon came to breathe a sigh of relief. Maybe I didn't have to be quite so perfect.

College allowed me the first real freedom of my life, and I began to separate from my overly protective parents. I began to figure out who I was as a person; in the past, I had always been told who I was. For the first two-and-a-half years, I lived either in the dorm or in an apartment by myself. It was heaven. I could just be with my own thoughts.

In my junior year of college, my Dad lost his civilian job— he had retired from the army some years before. Since my Dad had still been working on the military base doing what he did in the army, this meant he had to find a job in the private sector. There were no good options in the country, so my parents began to move to Austin, where I was attending college. Since they were paying for my education, this meant that I would be living with my father again while he found a job.

It didn't take long for my anger to show up. Everything about living at home again frustrated me. Dad threw a frozen chicken across the room when I said I wanted to be a vegetarian. Dad berated me for protesting the first Iraq war. I tried to share some of what I learned in classes, which contradicted some of the things I had always accepted as true, which prompted Dad to scream at me and tell me that now that I was going to college, I guess I thought I was smarter than he was.

These events just confused me. Dad had always been rageful and would say hurtful things, but in the past I had not thought much about the substance of his words. But now, as a young adult, the things he said did not make sense. I decided I would only discuss "safe" subjects with him, which narrowed the list pretty sharply: computers, science fiction books, and airplanes (which he adored, but which bored me to tears).

In my twenties came the first real breaks in the Family Mythology. I moved in with a man at 22—mostly because it was better than moving in with my parents again—and then I married him at 24. He couldn't stand my parents, which was a new perspective for me: weren't they perfect? How could he feel that way?

In retrospect, it is not surprising that my husband and I attracted one another. We were both only children, and he had cut off his parents before I met him (he was 17 years older than I was). He told me about his parents, and I had to admit they sounded pretty toxic: a rageful father and a passive-aggressive, controlling mother. At that time, I thought cutting them off completely was extreme, but I respected that it was his decision. As I began the slow process of understanding how similarly toxic my own parents were, however, I developed more compassion and understanding for his experience.

Awareness did not happen overnight. But during these years, I realized that I couldn't be in the same room with my parents for more than ten minutes without becoming seethingly angry.

On a number of occasions, I tried to express my feelings to my parents—I felt belittled, disrespected, and unheard. And they responded as they always had: "No, you don't. You don't feel that way. We don't mean it that way, so you can't possibly feel that way." Or, to use my mother's favorite phrase whenever I objected to something she said to me, "Don't get your panties in a bunch." As you might imagine, their assurances that I couldn't possibly feel what I felt did not help me to stop feeling these things. Instead, I became angrier.

Still, they let me know that my anger was completely unjustified—after all, there was no reason to be mad at them! *They* had no problems. *They* were tranquil. *They* were perfect. So the message was clear: if I was angry, there was clearly something wrong with *me*. I believed them, but it didn't make my anger go away.

In my late twenties, I began to visit healers who commented on the amount of sadness and grief I was holding inside. This made no sense at all to me. I was happy. I didn't feel sad or depressed. Yet, they would work on me, and I would cry. I felt it then. One actually asked me, "Who did this to you?" I had no idea what she was talking about. I had perfect parents. They couldn't have done anything to me. What was all this?

In my mid-thirties, my husband and I moved to Oregon. My parents did their best to get in the way of this move, but I actually liked the idea of having some distance from them. When we got here, however, my life changed completely.

Within a short space of time, I met Ahnna, who quickly became my best friend. Before long, we realized we were more than friends. We realized we were in love. That was hard. I was always gay-friendly, but I knew that in my family being a lesbian was not what was expected of me as a perfect child. I struggled with internal homophobia I didn't know I had. I knew that my parents would disapprove, and my own inner child had internalized that for herself. I had to re-evaluate my life. Had I always been a lesbian? If so, how could I not have known this? And the answer came: because you didn't want to know it. Ouch. This is when my blinders came off.

I left my husband, which I knew had been inevitable even before I met Ahnna. She was just the catalyst for my leaving a marriage that had ended years before. Still, it was hard. I didn't want to hurt him. I also didn't want to hurt me—and that was the Next Hard Thing. I had to tell my parents.

When I called my parents, I said I had left my husband, but I didn't say much more than that. My mother hated him, and now she felt she could fly to Portland and bring me home again to move in next door to her, so she came pretty quickly. When she met Ahnna, whom she thought was just a friend, my mother thanked her for "giving me my daughter back." Oh, boy.

After a couple of days, I took mom for a hike, and then I told her the truth. Suddenly, the weather changed completely. It was decidedly chilly...

"It's just a phase. It will end eventually. I don't think you're a lesbian. My advice is to stay in the closet. Don't tell your Dad."

Talk like this infuriated me. Here was Mom, telling me how I felt and who I was—again. It didn't seem to matter that her beliefs did not match my reality. I disputed her view of How Things Were, and she denied and argued, no matter what I said. There was no final, perfect argument that I could provide to make it stop. And I became angrier and angrier.

When Mom returned to Texas, all subsequent conversations with her centered on this subject in some way. She worked very hard to find an argument to make me see that I was not being perfect, and that I should change post-haste. She was also concerned that I not break this news to anyone else in our family, since that could reflect poorly on her.

Eventually, however, I did tell anyone who asked, and I purposely told my father the truth. Mom was not happy and said that I had "blindsided her" in doing so. My cousin, the sister of that shameful boy with whom I had once played doctor, called me up and quoted Bible verses to me. Since they now knew, my mother was willing to rally the troops to her side. And this is when I began to realize that I was no longer the Golden Child.

Since I could not be perfect and wear the family mask, my mother shifted her tactics entirely: by degrees, I became the object of her loathing. She was convinced that I was "doing this" to spite her personally, but that I would get over it eventually. Still, as time passed and I refused to conform to what was expected of me, there had to be a new narrative that would explain *why* I was not behaving perfectly—one that would simultaneously protect and enshrine the perfection of my parents. *They* weren't the ones with the problem—I was. This meant that, in my parents' eyes, I was not in my right mind. I was depressed. Indeed, I must be crazy in some way. It was the only explanation, right?

I married Ahnna in 2004. My parents did not attend. "You didn't plan your wedding for our convenience," Mom said (they were invited in April to an August wedding). Our wedding apparently conflicted with their need to replace the roof on their house so they could sell it and move to the country again. That hurt.

But my marriage to Ahnna is what has helped my inner child come out. I began to realize that those feelings of sadness and grief that healers were pointing out to me years earlier were real. They were present in me. The veneer of calmness that I had learned from my mother was not really calm. I had simply chosen not to feel the painful feelings of my inner child. And yet, the anger she felt still came out whenever my mother, in particular, was in the room. For the first time in my life, I became emotionally aware of myself. I became aware of my core feelings. But I didn't understand them yet. Where did all that rage and sadness come from?

I knew my parents loved me, but during these years I became aware of how conditional that love really was. Yes, they loved me—as long as I was perfect. They loved me—if I was not a lesbian. They loved me—as long as I acted in ways that validated their beliefs. They loved me—as long as I reflected well on them. But the more I became aware of what truly made me happy, and the freer I became to express that, the less I validated my parents' beliefs and expectations. In other words, the more I healed myself and did the things that brought me joy and freedom, the unhappier my parents became with me.

Our children came late into our lives. I was 36 when I had our daughter. Until then, my parents had no interest in seeing or visiting us. But when I gave birth to a healthy baby, they were interested again. We welcomed them into our home on several different occasions over the course of two years, and each visit was worse than the one before.

They came for our daughter's first Christmas. On Christmas morning, we had it all planned out. We had chosen every gift very carefully. I wanted everyone to open them slowly, one at a time, so we could enjoy the moment for each person. My mother had other ideas. Before Ahnna could even join us, my mother was opening our daughter's presents for her. We both missed most of it. Within 15 minutes, all gifts (except ours) were opened without fanfare. Just like that, it was all over. Our daughter was overwhelmed, and we felt like we had missed it all. I felt really disrespected. It wouldn't be the last time.

We had a rule in our house: no TV when our daughter was awake. We did not want her exposed to it, and particularly not to anything beyond "Sesame Street." Since my dad is addicted to watching TV, this put a strain on things. On the last day of their visit, my parents wanted to videotape themselves with our daughter on the couch. The TV was on, so I asked them to turn it off. They didn't. They also didn't respond to my request. They just looked at me as if to say, "What are you going to do about it?" So I walked over to the TV and turned it off myself, then returned to the kitchen.

A few weeks after my parents left, they mailed us a DVD of the footage they had taken at our home. Included at the end was the footage of my parents, on the couch with our daughter— complaining about how awful I was for not letting them watch TV! In my younger days, I didn't really understand what "passive-aggressive" meant. Now I do. This was a textbook example.

After that visit with my parents, Ahnna suggested something to me that was a revelation. Ahnna is the daughter of a counselor and has spent many years as a social worker herself. She has also had experience with personality disorders, so she asked me if it had ever occurred to me that my mother might suffer from Narcissistic Personality Disorder (NPD). It had never occurred to me that my mother might have a mental illness, so I read up on the subject. I was amazed and relieved to discover that my mother had nearly every indicator of this disorder. This is when my world began to make sense.

My inner child had been raised by someone who is mentally ill, and who married someone who is a co-dependent enabler of her illness. My father is not mentally ill, but his own mother has many traits of NPD, although I do not think she actually has NPD. Still, it was easy to see that my father had essentially married his mother. And our Family Mythology—that we were all perfectly perfect—is actually an extension of my mother's mental illness. It goes without saying that a narcissist must believe in their own perfection above all else. As her child, I was an extension of her. But as I began to think and feel for myself—from her perspective, rebelling—her behavior became crazier and crazier. She was pulling out all of the stops to try to get me to "behave" and respond in a way that would validate her view of herself and her world. And the more she did this, the angrier I became.

It was a tremendous relief to have a reason for her behavior. It was a tremendous relief to know that it was not all about me being wrong or bad, or anything else. It was never about me. And yet—my inner child still had these ingrained beliefs that I was the problem, that I was the failure, and that I was not really worthy of love because I could not behave in a way that was contrary to my own nature. These were the roots of my sadness and grief. My inner child wanted to say, "This is who I am!" And when she tried, my mother said, "No, you are not! You are *this* way!"

When I stopped living a lie, my mother reacted with amazing ferocity and venom. Few things can match the rage of the invalidated narcissist. She tried everything to control my behavior, and I tried very hard to have a relationship with her anyway. I changed the way I talked. I was honest about my feelings. I used every tool I could find, but as my daughter reached the age where she could talk and interact, my mother began to see her as my replacement. I became the bad guy, the "bad mom," and Grammy was the good, loving one who would protect her from *mean old mommy.*

So what was Grammy protecting my daughter from? I wanted my daughter to nap. At two, she needed an afternoon nap. Of course, she was always good at keeping herself awake, but the rule was that she had to have "rest time" whether she slept or not. Mom said I was cruel.

I also wanted my daughter to feel free to express her feelings. But whenever she cried, my mother gave her food to quiet her. Suddenly, my lifelong weight problem made sense...

We also asked my mother not to do certain things, like not pulling my daughter by the arm. It's easy to dislocate a toddler's shoulder. She responded that it was okay, the doctor had showed her how to put it back, and she had done that for me many times. (I remember what a dislocated shoulder felt like, and it hurts.) We told her that was abusive, and we insisted that she stop doing it. She said we were treating her like a child. She told me that I was just like Hitler.

By this time, I certainly understood that my mother really did have a mental illness, but I thought I could work with it. She's my mom, right? These are her grandchildren. But I was no longer in the fold. Worse, I knew I could no longer depend on them, or even trust them. I had become the enemy.

When we moved in 2007, they came to help. Ahnna has a disability, and I had become very sick. I had already been to the hospital in an ambulance once when they arrived. I was on strong antibiotics.

The day after they arrived, I woke up and didn't feel right. I hadn't eaten much in days, so I thought maybe I just needed to eat something. Maybe my blood sugar was off. I went to the kitchen, fixed half a bagel, and took one bite. Whatever was wrong with me, it wasn't about food. An icy chill crept over me, and my vision started to go dark. I was about to pass out. I somehow made my way to a chair, and it took all of my willpower to remain upright. My mother told my dad to get me some orange juice. She sat on the couch with our daughter, who was also sick, in her arms.

Ahnna came into the living room, took one look at me, and asked if I could talk. I shook my head. Our land line had been disconnected already, so Ahnna asked my dad to hand her the cell phone so she could call 911. He picked it up and just held it. She had to ask him several times. Mom said I just needed orange juice. My lips, I am told, were turning blue.

My father eventually did relinquish the cell phone. The EMTs arrived and hooked me up to a heart monitor. I had tachycardia, and my heart was beating arhythmically. I was aware of my mother, sitting on the couch and rocking my daughter, apparently unconcerned, and I just knew that somewhere inside, it would be okay with her if I died so she could "get my daughter" (even though Ahnna legally adopted her, the narcissist in my mother would not see that as an impediment).

They put me in the ambulance, put me on oxygen, started an IV, and drove away. According to Ahnna, after the door closed, my mom said, "So, what are we having for breakfast?" Ahnna was in shock, but my mom sent my father to McDonald's for takeout. Afterward, Ahnna wanted to go to the hospital, but my mother said she couldn't be left alone in a house with no cleaning supplies, so she sent my father to the store for some Windex first. He was gone for two hours, during which time I had a medical procedure to get my heart to beat normally.

I was in good hands, fortunately, and eventually Ahnna and my father did come to the hospital. I was coming out of the anesthesia when they came into my room. Ahnna immediately started to cry, and my dad went to comfort her. I was still pretty weak and tired, but I wondered, "How come I don't get any comforting?"

This experience and many others with my parents finally opened my eyes. I could not trust them to have my back. If Ahnna had not been present, I would probably be dead. And the passive aggression, the control battles, the gaslighting—all of it was toxic. Whenever my parents left, it took weeks for our daughter and our whole family to regain our even keel. It was terrible. And now we had a son. It could not go on.

Not everyone who has toxic parents must cut them off, but for some people, it is the only solution. It was for me. But it is painful. I know my parents do not understand why this happened, and I cannot explain it to them. They would try to argue me into submission if I tried. And nothing would change. Nothing *can* change. My mother is mentally ill. She will always be mentally ill. I still love my parents, but I am happier without them in my life. My family is happier without the never-ending toxic behaviors that I saw play out in my own home the last time they were here. It is just not acceptable to me. This is my boundary.

Still, most people did not understand my boundary. I could see the wheels turning in their minds: "What kind of a person cuts off her own parents? There must be something wrong with you." Meeting or knowing my parents did not help to clarify this for family outsiders, either. People with personality disorders can be perfectly charming, narcissists particularly so. And the Mask of

Perfection—the Family Myth that gets shown to the world—is very convincing. From the perspective of outsiders, why, these people *are* the perfect parents. They *do* have the perfect house. They *must* be pillars of the community. For people who either could not see past the mask, or who simply did not want to understand my reasons, I was the bad guy. I was the troubled one, the depressed one, the crazy one.

I accepted that some people would leave my life, but I was encouraged and gratified to see the new people who were coming into my life. Amazing, loving, supportive people. Finally!

My inner child is grateful for not having to constantly defend herself from my parents and some of my extended family, but she still has toxic patterning to work out. She has learned a lot, however. She learned that she had suppressed her emotions. She learned what those emotions are and why they are there. She learned how to process them so that they can be released. She learned how to make new, healthier choices for herself and her family. She learned that it is possible to find joy. And in the process, she is learning who she really is, instead of playing a role that someone else has defined for her.

Discovering your inner child is a journey into discovering who you really are. Once you begin to peel away the masks and understand the toxic patterns that affect your life even now, you can begin to make new choices. Healing is a process, and you can learn to choose joy.

This book captures what I have learned while healing my own inner child. I am not a clinical therapist. I have no degree in psychology. I am simply a healer who has worked long and hard to heal herself. It has been an incredible journey of discovery, and even though I have had painful moments, I learned from them, and the result is joy. I am happier than I have ever been in my life. I have everything that I need. I have the love of friends and family—a family of my own creation and choosing.

By including my own story here, I hope to illustrate that healing really is a process. I did not find my joy overnight. I was clueless, confused, and frequently stumped. How was I supposed to get over these hurdles? What was the problem? Keep at it, whatever you do. Please do not give up. I went from being clueless to aware to capable of making new choices to joyful. So can you.

In this book, I make reference to Spirit—specifically, your Spirit, for that is the most important one. Your Spirit was made in the image of whatever you think is divine in this Universe; therefore, you are also divine. It is my hope that you can become best friends with your inner child, who will help you discover your Spirit and the things that bring you joy.

This revised and expanded edition of the book includes a new chapter about inner child archetypes, an expanded chapter about abuse and common toxic behaviors, and a new chapter about learning to love yourself, which can be one of the greatest challenges that people face when working to heal their inner child.

I want to thank the people who have supported me on this journey: my beautiful wife, Ahnna Hawkesworth; my beautiful daughter, Wren; my handsome young son, Harry; our children's godparents: Lana Lyons, Lyra Hall, and Tessa Swigart; David Maynard, Thomas TenEyck, David French, and particularly, all of the people who have written to share their stories with me. I am so glad to have been of service.

And lastly, I want to thank the people who helped me become the person I am today. Without this journey, this book would never have been written. I am thankful for that. So, to my parents: thank you, from afar. To my ex-husband, who is also the product of toxic parents: thank you. And to my extended family, who has judged me and found me wanting: thank you. All of you, in your own way, have helped me to understand what conditional love looks like, so that now I can choose unconditional love.

Who is your inner child?

Adults are obsolete children.
—Dr. Seuss

A grown-up is a child with layers on.
—Woody Harrelson

Your inner child is your core emotional being, the "person" who shares your body with you and who can respond to situations before your grown-up self even has a chance to think about it. This core self determines how you behave in relationships, with your children, with your parents, and even on the job. In other words, it shows up any time your emotions are involved—which is all the time.

Your inner ruler

What would happen if children ran the world? What if grown-ups threw a tantrum every time something did not go their way? What if we just took what we wanted from other people, whenever we wanted it? What if we resolved our differences by hitting or calling each other names? What if we decided we were only going to play all day?

There are many wonderful things about children and your inner child, but it is probably not a good idea to let them run the world. For example, playing is something we should all do, but sooner or later, some work must be done. As adults, we can balance the needs of our inner child with the needs of others.

Of course, you have probably encountered some grown-ups who *do* behave like children, and that is their inner child talking. Your inner child should be a blessing, not a tyrant. You must do the work to recognize, honor, and reparent your inner child, or he or she will run your life. A healed inner child can lead you to your joy; a wounded inner child will cause you to replay your wounds over and over again.

Your inner child's coping strategies

When you were growing up, you learned how to respond and interact with the world from the people around you. You learned to emulate the behaviors and emotional patterns that your parents and family learned from their parents and family before them. Some of these patterns are helpful; some are not. But you learned them at such a young age that they became ingrained in your nervous system. When you repeat a pattern often enough, it becomes automatic.

Your inner child is just that—a child. A slight or event that may sound trivial to an adult can be a big deal to a child. A child's world needs to feel safe. They need the security of feeling loved, of being given appropriate boundaries, and feeling accepted for who they are. Unfortunately, not all children feel safe, so they develop strategies for coping with their environment and the world. Some strategies may include:

- **Going undercover**
  The inner child may feel safest if they can emulate what they *think* their parents and others want. This generally involves hiding who they really are and pretending to be the child that they believe their guardians want.

- **Becoming invisible**

  In order to feel safe, a child may find that "flying under the radar" is the best strategy. If no one sees them, then there is no problem.

- **Stuffing emotions**

  If a child's world is not safe, they will have feelings about that. They will probably feel anger (an emotion that includes frustration, resentment, and depression), sadness, and grief (because they are mourning the fact that some basic needs were not met). These are big, scary emotions for a child to handle on their own, so if a child feels particularly unsafe, they may decide that the best course is not to feel anything at all, so they work to block their emotions. Most addictions have their root in stuffing emotions. We may literally stuff them with food, alcohol, tobacco, or other drugs.

These or any other coping strategies become automatic after awhile, so you continue to implement them long after you have grown up, even if you now live in a safer environment. The problem with continuing these or other harmful behaviors is that they cause you to live out of integrity with who you really are, which makes it impossible for you to find happiness.

If you continue to use these coping strategies, your grown-up self may experience the following results:

- **Not knowing who you really are**

  The problem with spending most of your childhood undercover is that you begin to believe your own deception, and you forget the authentic self that you were trying to hide. As a result, you end up living someone else's life instead of your own, and you may spend years wondering why you are unhappy.

- **Becoming accustomed to being invisible**
  If you became a master of not being seen, then you became accustomed to it. This has many ramifications for your adult self, including:

  - *Not getting recognized for your work or contributions.* This can have a negative impact on your career, and failure to be recognized for good work can make you feel resentful and negatively impact your self-esteem.

  - *Becoming uncomfortable in intimate relationships.* The purpose of intimate relationships is to be able to share yourself with another person who hopefully loves and accepts you just as you are. In order for that to work, you have to feel comfortable showing your significant other your authentic self. In other words, you have to let them see you. If you prefer being invisible, being seen can feel overwhelming and cause you to sabotage your relationships.

  - *Feeling isolated or alone.* If you are invisible, you cannot connect with other people, and you may feel like people reject you. In reality, they probably are not rejecting you—they just do not see you because your strategy was so effective.

- **Forgetting how to feel**
  When you stuff your emotions, you do it because you subconsciously do not want to feel the so-called "negative" emotions: anger, sadness, grief, and others. Unfortunately, turning off these emotions means that you turn off *all* emotions, so you cannot experience happiness, love, or joy, either. Addiction issues make

this worse: if you become addicted to a substance, your emotional development stops, because you are using the substance to avoid dealing with your emotions. Any recovery from addiction means that you must resume dealing with your emotions again and pick up where you left off.

Until you understand your inner child issues, you may not recognize that your behaviors are not serving you, or that you are unhappy. It is very common to feel frustrated and angry with yourself for not understanding why you act or react the way you do, or to wonder why your life isn't going the way you want it to. An unhealed inner child can make you a master at beating yourself up, which does not solve anything. Instead, you feel like a failure for reliving another "failed" relationship or reacting "that way" again, whether the response is tears, anger, self-sabotage, or any other negative outcome.

So what can you do about your inner child? Why does it continually act out when you don't want it to? Why can't you just act like a grown-up?

The answer lies in understanding, loving, and healing your inner child.

To heal is to make happy.
—A Course in Miracles

Meeting your inner child

In every real man a child is hidden that wants to play.
—Friedrich Nietzsche

You can heal your inner child and help it to "grow up," but you have to be willing to do the work. The first step is to meet your inner child and acknowledge what it wants and needs. Then you can begin the process of reparenting your inner child, and reparenting yourself.

It's very important to treat your inner child with the respect and love that it deserves. You have spent your entire life treating your inner child—yourself—very harshly. You have told him or her that they are a failure, that they are powerless, that they are unworthy, that they are stupid or ugly, or whatever horrible thing you have ever told yourself. Let that stop now.

The following meditation will help you to see your inner child in a new way. I recommend doing this more than once; you are likely to learn something new about your inner child every time you do this. Healing the inner child is a process, and as you proceed, you will become aware of what the issues are. However, *realizing* that you have an issue does not mean that you have *healed* the issue. The realization is just the beginning.

Prepare for the meditation

Sit in a comfortable chair and relax. Take at least seven deep breaths, inhaling through the nose, and exhaling forcefully through the mouth. Mentally ask Spirit to cut any cords that are blocking your healing for this issue. Also ask Spirit to assist you in the meditation. Take a few moments and feel it come in for you and comfort you.

Meditation: Meet your inner child

See yourself sitting in a comfortable chair in a warm, sunny room. The windows are open, and you can hear the sound of birds singing outside the window. The scent of your favorite flowers is in the air.

As you look around the room, you see that you are in a child's play room. A shelf is filled with all of your favorite children's books. Toys that you recognize from your childhood are neatly stowed around the room. There is a child-sized table in one corner, littered with crayons and coloring books.

The door to the play room opens, and a child peeks in at you. You recognize that this is your inner child. Ask him or her to come in. Tell them that they are safe here.

Ask them, "What is your name?"

As the child begins to play, look at them and see them with all of the issues and traits that you dislike in yourself. How does this make you feel? Whatever your feelings are, honor them for a few moments.

Next to you on a small table lies a magic wand. Pick it up. This wand has the power to remove negativity from all things. Point it at your inner child and say, "Show me who you really are."

A beam of pink energy flows from the wand to your inner child, covering them from head to toe. As you watch, this pink energy removes all of the issues, imperfections, and traits that you dislike about yourself. These things float away from your inner child easily, revealing the Spirit and true identity of the person beneath them.

What do you see?

What feelings come up about your inner child? What memories?

Ask your inner child how old they are, and then wait for the answer.

Ask them how they feel right now, and then wait for the answer.

Ask your inner child what you need to do help them feel safe, and then wait for the answer.

Open your arms to your inner child and ask them to come to you. Hold them and say, "I owe all that I am to you, and I thank you for that. But I am a grown up, and I will take care of you now. I love you, and you are safe."

As you hold your inner child, Archangel Gabriel sits with you and takes both of you in her arms. She cares for you in the same way that you will now care for your inner child. Receive her love, compassion, and comfort, and then share it with your inner child.

When you are ready, ask your inner child what they would like to do today, and then honor that.

After the meditation

I highly recommend journaling your thoughts, feelings, and experiences.

Know that all of the things that were removed by your magic wand are not really part of you. The magic wand simply helps to reveal the real you. Can you have compassion for your child self and what they have experienced? Can you love your child self?

It is a good idea to do this meditation on a regular basis, at least at first. Your inner child may have a hard time trusting you, and the more you work with him or her, the better your results will be. Try this meditation once a week, and talk to your inner child daily to reassure and love them.

3

The world according to your inner child

Grown-ups never understand anything for themselves, and it is tiresome for children to be always and forever explaining things to them.
—Antoine de Saint-Exupéry

It is important to understand that, while your inner child *is* you, he or she does not *think* like you do. Your rational, adult brain thinks in a more mature way, integrating your years of knowledge and experience. Your inner child does not think rationally; instead, he or she thinks emotionally. This is why it feels like no matter what you do, you cannot change anything. Thought does not enter into it—feelings do. But when you come to understand your inner child's feelings and motivations, you can create strategies to re-pattern yourself and make the changes that are necessary for a happy life.

Emotional patterns that your inner child learned

Ultimately, you learned how to feel from your parents or guardians. If your parents were not comfortable with their emotions, then you probably are not, either. If your parents suppressed their emotions, you probably do also. Learned emotional responses are generational, and the chain can only be broken when someone decides to heal them.

It is often helpful to start by recognizing what the emotional patterns in your family are. If you can understand this mentally, then with some work, you can start to integrate the knowledge emotionally. This is a process that takes time, gentleness, and courage.

To start, ask your inner child some questions about the way emotions were presented or expressed in your home. One method is to interview your inner child.

Exercise: Interviewing your inner child

- What would you say your emotional state generally is?

- What would you say your emotional state generally is when you are under stress?

- Do you prefer to avoid confrontation or arguments?

- If a confrontation or argument takes place, what role do you play?

- Were you teased or ridiculed if you cried?

- If you saw a parent crying and asked them about it, how did they respond?

- When a pet or loved one died, how was grief expressed in your home?

- If you made a mistake, how did your parents react?

- Was it okay to be silly?

- Did your parents smile?

- Did your parents laugh?

- How did you play?

- What sorts of play and activities were "off limits" and why?

- What feelings made your family members uncomfortable?

- What was the dominant mood in the house?

The answers to these questions will lead to more questions, which will illuminate how your inner child responds emotionally. This process will also help you understand what your inner child is really feeling and what emotions you have been avoiding. Repressed emotion is not unfelt; it is just repressed. Emotion is a powerful energy, and if we bottle it up instead of feeling it, it causes us real harm, energetically and in our relationships and lives. For example, people with a lot of repressed anger are often unaware (in denial) that they are angry, but this unprocessed feeling rules everything in their lives. This can be healed, but the first step is to acknowledge the anger.

When you live with unexpressed emotions for a long time, it feels normal, even comfortable. Learning to feel your emotions and release them can make you very uncomfortable, because it does not feel the way you are accustomed to feeling. Paradoxically, joy, happiness, love, and peace can feel very painful at first because they are unfamiliar. With time and gentleness, however, you can become comfortable with love and happiness and let go of any learned need for negativity.

Your inner child's feelings

Emotions are a vital part of human experience. Without them, you cannot fully participate in the world, find joy, or connect with other people or Spirit. And yet, many people make an unconscious decision early in their lives to cut off or avoid their emotions. The reasons are many:

- Abuse (physical, mental, emotional, sexual)
- Toxic or mentally ill parents
- Traumatic experience
- Feeling unsafe

- Difficulty trusting others

Certainly, people sometimes experience great pain, and who wants to feel that? And if you are faced with pain on a regular basis (in an abusive home, for example), your inner child's decision to stop feeling is born of self-preservation: you, the child, literally cannot cope with what is happening, so you shut down a part of your mental, emotional, and spiritual self because the physical reality is too overwhelming.

Your inner child's emotions, however, are the key to your healing and your happiness. Shutting down or avoiding your emotions cuts you off from *all* emotions, including joy and contentment.

The primary challenge for people who have chosen not to feel is to realize that they have even made this unconscious decision. No one is aware of making the decision to bail on their emotions, and many people mistake a life without feelings for happiness, because they do not know what real happiness feels like. How do you heal this?

Answer these questions:

- When asked how you feel, do you generally respond (sincerely) that you are happy, or "fine?"

- In general, would you say that you never or seldom get angry with other people?

- Would you say that your emotional state is generally "calm?"

- Do you prefer to avoid confrontation or arguments?

- If a confrontation or argument takes place, do you play the role of peacekeeper?

If you answered yes to three or more of these questions, you may be trying to prevent yourself from feeling your emotions. But the truth is, no one ever successfully cuts off their feelings.

You will still feel them; they are just bottled up inside and remain unexpressed, which creates the illusion that you are calm, peaceful, and happy, even when the opposite is true.

This illusion is not designed to convince others, however. It is primarily designed to convince *you*, because the moment you start to acknowledge your true feelings, you will have to face your own pain so that you can transmute it. This is the art of healing.

What your inner child hears

No two people interpret what is said to them in quite the same way. The words may be exactly the same, but the meaning we take from them can differ wildly. And if our interpretations of what is said differ enough, we cannot communicate well or at all. Misunderstandings and hurt feelings arise more often because we hear things differently, rather than from malicious intent.

> *Offense taken is worse than offense given.*
> —Orin, as channeled through Sanaya Roman

You have probably found that there are people who seem to understand you, and then there are people with whom you are always communicating poorly. Whatever the issue is, you can never seem to "get" these people, or they can't seem to "get" you. What is going on here? Why is it so hard?

As you grew up, your inner child learned a specific way of communicating. You may have learned healthy ways to communicate, toxic ways to communicate, or a little of both. But just as importantly, you learned a certain way of *hearing* what is said to you. The information that you receive comes through the filter of your inner child. This filter is emotionally based and not terribly rational. In fact, the conscious mind is seldom aware that this filter exists at all, yet it is the most important factor in how you communicate with others, and it determines to a large extent whether your relationships are happy or not.

When you hear or read something, the information passes through your inner child's filter. This filter consists of a set of secret rules of behavior, including how you react to things. It looks for patterns based on the events of your past and tries to match what is heard with incidents from your past. When it finds what feels like a match, you react to what was said on the basis of what happened to you in the past, even if it does not have any bearing on the current situation.

For example, if you felt criticized growing up, your filter will be hyper-sensitive to anything that feels like criticism. Someone might say to you, "That dinner you made was delicious! The only thing missing was a good bottle of wine." Instead of hearing the compliment, your filter might focus on what was missing and interpret what was said as, "If you were a really good host you would have served wine with the meal," with the result that you feel hurt. Whether you respond angrily or bite your lip and swallow your feelings, the other person is likely to feel confused by your response. As a result, communication between you has just broken down.

Your filters are firmly rooted in your past, and this is why it is so important to heal your past. Everything you hear, think, do, and say is influenced by the emotions and wounds of your past. If you do not heal this, you keep repeating the patterns that hurt you, over and over again. Of course, this does not mean that you must forget the past; that is not possible. Instead, you must release it and turn your attention forward. How do you do this?

You can change the past by changing how you think about the past. You can look at the things that happened to you and feel like a victim, or you can take responsibility for the things you have control over: namely, your thoughts, actions, and reactions. The simple act of *deciding* not to be a victim is powerful in itself. The act of deciding to forgive yourself for what happened to you in the past is also immensely powerful.

Forgiving yourself and your inner child opens all doors to healing. You do not have to do any of this "perfectly." There is no single formula for healing. But if you shift your attention from what is behind you to what is here now and what lies ahead of you, you will discover where you true power is. It is here now, with each thought that you give energy to, with each emotion that you allow yourself to feel, and with each choice that you make.

The next time you feel hurt by something that was said, ask yourself this question: "Are they trying to hurt me, or is that feeling coming from my inner child?" The answer will help you identify what your inner child is trying to tell you and give you the opportunity to heal it.

Learned responses and your nervous system

When you teach your son, you teach your son's son.
—The Talmud

The way we respond emotionally and socially is trained into our bodies by repeated exposure and action. Some of the ways we learn to respond and react are positive; some are negative. Some are a little of both.

For example, if you had a parent with obsessive-compulsive disorder (OCD), you know that this behavior is not a healthy way to be. However, certain aspects of this disorder—like attention to detail and ability to focus—can be good in moderation. But if you learned the obsessive-compulsive way of doing things as a child, then by the time you're an adult, your body wants to do it that way *all the time*. It is a learned behavior, so it will take conscious effort on your part to relax more and let things go when you need to.

Your inner child learned your family's way of responding to the world—for better or worse. And the more you do something, the better you get at doing it. If you learned early on that screaming was the most effective way to be heard (or the only way to be heard), then your body learned to respond that way automatically. Thought does not enter into it.

Your nervous system is infinitely trainable, and the pathways you exercised or observed the most as a child are the ones that you are most likely to speed down as an adult. Since our behavior becomes automatic, we tend to believe that there is little we can do about it, even when we know that the behavior is toxic or produces unwanted results. But the good news is: your nervous system *is* infinitely trainable, and you *can* do something about it.

Mental and emotional patterns

When you were a child, you learned how to function in the world you were given. You learned what things were rewarded and what things were punished. You learned which choices brought pleasure to you or your parents, and you learned which choices did not. Based on these experiences, you created a system of value judgments that more or less mirrored what you learned from your environment.

In your emotional world, you learned which feelings were okay to express in your home. You also learned which feelings were not welcome. And you developed an emotional framework that you hoped would protect you from the hurts that you encountered in the world.

Together, these mental and emotional patterns dictate how you interact with the world and how you live your life. None of this is "bad" or "wrong;" it just is. It's what happens when a human being grows up in the world.

Your inner child is primarily motivated by the following goals:

- To be safe

- To be validated and heard

- To be loved

All human beings are searching for these things. Your mental and emotional patterning is an inexperienced attempt by your young child self to gain or protect these things. This is completely understandable.

As an adult, however, the mental and emotional patterns that your two- to six-year-old self created are not going to serve you, particularly when your body has learned to act on them without any direction from your adult mind.

So, what causes your body's nervous system to respond? When do your mental and emotional patterns come into play?

Emotional triggers

If you observe yourself as you go about your daily business, you will probably find that there are long stretches of time when the Grown-Up is in charge, and things are going smoothly. This generally happens when you are in your routine, nothing unexpected is happening, and you are emotionally calm. So far, so good.

But then something might happen: a delay, a crisis, a perceived slight, and all of a sudden, your inner child is running the show. You've been down this road before, and you know what to expect: you may behave in a way you will regret later, you will end up feeling bad about yourself, or things just won't be resolved in a way that makes you happy. Why does this keep happening?

Your inner child takes over when you encounter an *emotional trigger*. An emotional trigger is a feeling or experience that you unconsciously associate with any of these fears:

- Not feeling safe

- Not feeling validated or heard

- Not feeling loved

When something happens that "feels like" a match with a past feeling or experience, your inner child automatically assumes that what is happening now is a replay of that past incident. The more painful your memory is, the more ardently your inner child will attempt to protect him- or herself from it.

Emotional triggers can take many forms. Sometimes all it takes is for someone to say something to you: the words that were chosen, the tone, or the circumstances can all combine to remind you of a painful pattern from your past, with the result that you lash out in anger or shut down resentfully, depending on what your inner child learned to do in response to this situation.

Your fears are your primary emotional triggers, and your inner child's responses in the face of them can be quite complex. For example, let's say that you have a pattern of failed relationships. If your worst fear is to be rejected or abandoned by people who mean something to you, your emotional triggers may ensure precisely this outcome. How?

If your inner child feels rejected or abandoned—physically, emotionally, or spiritually—then your inner child assumes that this will keep happening. He or she *expects* to match that pattern. And one thing is certain: if you expect to match your patterns, you will. This is how your thoughts create your world.

In this example, your inner child expects rejection, so it will create that reality in a couple of ways. First, your inner child will guide you to form relationships with people who are most likely to reject you. (If your inner child feels rejected by your father, and you are a woman, then you may unconsciously seek out men like your father in relationships.) Another way in which your inner child might create havoc is to assume that all "good" people are going to reject you anyway, so he or she may decide to beat them to the punch and reject *them* first. To a young child, the best way to avoid emotional pain in this scenario is not to get too close to anyone. Trust is a huge issue, and your inner child can be a mastermind at self-sabotage, leaving your adult mind wondering why you never seem to have a close relationship with anybody.

Shame

> *The difference between guilt and shame is very clear—in theory. We feel guilty for what we do. We feel shame for what we are.*
> —Lewis B. Smedes

Everyone experiences shame. As children, we are taught that some things are okay, and some things are not. In fact, we are told that some things are truly, exceptionally horrible. And if those horrible things happen to be a part of us, we begin to think that *we* are horrible.

Shame is a big deal to your inner child, and it doesn't matter if the thing you are ashamed of is "big" or "little." To a child, shame is a huge issue, and it can run your life.

It is important to understand your shame so that you can heal it. Ask yourself some questions:

- Were you taught that sexual feelings were dirty or shameful?

- Were you taught that parts of your body were dirty or shameful?

- What kind of behaviors were you shamed out of? Did you understand why these behaviors were considered bad?

- Were you criticized for looking or dressing a certain way?

- Were you criticized for being unable to excel at an activity that your parents thought was important?

- Did you feel stupid or inadequate as a child?

- Did someone abuse you when you were a child? If so, did you believe it was your fault?

If you answered yes to any of these, you have discovered a pathway to your original shame. These questions are hardly comprehensive, however. Humans are very good at finding ways to feel shame, and there is probably more than one doorway into yours.

When you understand your inner child's shame, you can begin the healing process. Seeing and acknowledging it allows your adult mind to understand it. This is very important. When you understand it mentally, you can begin the work to understand it emotionally.

Inner child archetypes

Your inner child deserves all of the love and compassion that every child in this world deserves, but it can be difficult at first to envision a part of yourself as a child. You may be so accustomed to replaying the mental tapes of how bad you are that your child self seems unreachable.

But if you start to think about the other kids you knew when you were growing up, you may notice a tendency to group these many personalities into "characters" that are familiar to you. In one set of groupings, you may have the jocks, the popular kids, the "brains," and the geeks. This is an oversimplification, of course, and every person has their own special set of circumstances and characteristics that makes them truly unique. Nevertheless, archetypes can be useful in helping you to understand and have compassion for your inner child.

As you read the descriptions of the archetypes in the following sections, you may find that your inner child bears a strong resemblance to one or more of these, and you may have traits from several of them. There is no hard and fast rule here. If you recognize any of these archetypes in yourself, please do not judge yourself harshly. There is nothing wrong with your child self finding a way to cope and remain safe. Your job now is to understand why this happened so that you can heal it.

The Tough Kid

Also known as: The Loner

The Tough Kid spends most of their energy showing the world that nothing bothers them. Nothing can penetrate their veneer. Like a duck, any opinion or criticism just slides right off their back and into the pond. "I'm rubber, and you're glue, and whatever you say bounces off of me and sticks to you."

The worst thing that can happen to the Tough Kid is for someone else to witness a display of emotion, no matter how tiny. To be caught crying is a disaster. To be seen feeling *anything* results in shame because the Tough Kid believes in their core that feelings are a sign of weakness which other people will use against them.

The Tough Kid's true feelings

The truth is that the Tough Kid feels a lot. In fact, they may be *more* sensitive than the average kid, but they learned early on that it was not safe to show it. They may have been ridiculed for their feelings, or they may have been teased for them by people who were uncomfortable with these feelings. Whatever the cause, the Tough Kid decided that it was better not to show the world how they really felt because they did not want their feelings to be used against them.

How the Tough Kid rules your life

If your inner child is the Tough Kid, then hiding your emotions is your biggest priority. In effect, you have attempted to shut off your feelings, which means you do not feel anything—good or bad. The big problem here is not so much that you have hidden your feelings from the world, but that you have hidden them from yourself. You do not want to acknowledge them in any form because they are painful, and you are actually quite sensitive. Because you feel things so intensely, you are afraid that facing your feelings will blow your world apart.

Another important driver for you is shame. You work hard to hide your feelings because you fear the shame of having a witness to them. You fear that your feelings will betray you in some way and make others see you as weak or imperfect, which will allow them to take advantage of you.

Healing the Tough Kid

In a way, the Tough Kid does what the Old Lady who Swallowed a Fly does—swallowing bigger and bigger feelings to keep them all at bay. But it all began with the first feeling:

> *I know an old lady who swallowed a fly,*
> *I don't know why she swallowed the fly,*
> *I guess she'll die.*

To get the fly, she swallowed more and more animals, each increasingly larger than the one before, until:

> *I know an old lady who swallowed a cow,*
> *I wonder how she swallowed a cow?!*
> *She swallowed the cow to catch the goat,*
> *She swallowed the goat to catch the dog,*
> *She swallowed the dog to catch the cat,*
> *She swallowed the cat to catch the bird,*
> *She swallowed the bird to catch the spider,*
> *That wriggled and jiggled and tickled inside her,*
> *She swallowed the spider to catch the fly,*
> *I don't know why she swallowed the fly,*
> *I guess she'll die.*
>
> *I know an old lady who swallowed a horse,*
> *She's dead, of course!!*

The Tough-Kid act is just as hard to maintain the longer you try to keep it up, and while it may not physically kill you, it is an emotional death that will keep you miserable.

It is vitally important to be able to recognize and honor your true feelings. Without this, you cannot find happiness. To get there, you have to face the shame that has driven you into hiding. When you were little, you protected yourself from too much exposure, and that is okay. But now you are a grown-up, and you can reassure your tough inner child that the only opinion about your feelings that matters is yours.

There is no weakness in feeling; the ability to feel is a strength. Your world will not collapse because you allow yourself to feel strong emotion. This is the key to your prison. Think about all the time and energy you expend trying to keep your feelings bottled up inside and trying to avoid exposure. It will take time to convince your inner child that it is safe to be seen emotionally, but start with the following affirmation.

Affirmation:

My feelings are messengers that help me navigate my life. It is now safe for me to feel them and express them.

The Invisible Kid

Also known as: The Weird Kid, The Quiet Kid

"Do you remember that kid who always sat in the back of class? What was his name?" The Invisible Kid excels at flying under the radar. Their hair, their dress, their posture, everything about them says, "You don't see me. I'm invisible. Move along."

There is safety in anonymity, according to the Invisible Kid. It is far better not to be seen because if you *are* seen, bad things will probably happen to you. People might want to get close to you, and really, it's just easier if they keep their distance. The

Invisible Kid will never be popular, but they never expected to be popular anyway. They *do* expect to be hurt or rejected, though, and who wants to go there?

The Invisible Kid's true feelings

The Invisible Kid feels fundamentally unsafe in the world. They probably experienced some toxic behaviors at home, even if they cannot identify just what those are. Primarily, the Invisible Kid is afraid to be noticed. If someone notices them, then they might be rejected, berated, ridiculed, or worse.

There are many tools that the Invisible Kid employs to maintain their camouflage. Physically, their hair may obscure much of their face; they may slouch; they may choose inconspicuous, dark clothing; and they may (unconsciously) gain weight. Emotionally, they keep their cards very close to their vest. Sharing their thoughts and feelings with someone else may be difficult. They may talk little, fearing that someone will criticize what they say. In addition, talking "gives them away" and might let someone else see who they really are, and that does not feel safe.

How the Invisible Kid rules your life

If your inner child is the Invisible Kid, then you have worked hard not to be seen, and unfortunately, you have probably been wildly successful. As a result, you feel isolated and unappreciated, because no one can see the real you. The downside to invisibility is that you miss out on true intimacy and get overlooked in your job and at home. People literally overlook your contributions and accomplishments and seldom take your needs and wants into account, largely because they do not know what they are.

Healing the Invisible Kid

The Invisible Kid is very distant:

Twinkle, twinkle, little star,
How I wonder what you are!
Up above the world so high
Like a diamond in the sky.
Twinkle, twinkle, little star,
How I wonder what you are!

To heal, you will need to coax your inner child back down to earth. You are indeed a diamond, so bring your brilliance closer and let it shine! How can anyone know you if you do not give them a chance? Let your inner child know that you are in charge now, and that you will take care of them.

Like the Tough Kid, it will take time to convince your inner child that it is safe to be seen. After all, being seen is scary, and it makes you feel vulnerable. But you have power within that you can draw on.

Affirmation:

I am loved, I am valued, and I matter. It is now safe for me to be seen. I am a powerful person.

The Bad Kid

Also known as: The Delinquent, The Troublemaker, The Stupid Kid

The Bad Kid is very, very bad. They believe they were born that way, and this belief is reinforced everywhere they turn: by their parents, by their teachers, and by the other kids. Being bad is the only thing that has ever gotten them any attention, and being scowled at or disapproved of by any adult feels like victory.

The Bad Kid is certain that no one can love them because they are so bad, and they set out to prove this daily. Whether they are proving this to a parent or a partner, if their behavior is met with love or tolerance, they are pretty certain that they can eventually elicit what they believe are the *true* feelings of their loved ones: abhorrence and disgust. If anyone dares to say, "I will love you no matter what," the Bad Kid responds with, "Want to bet?"

The Bad Kid's true feelings

The Bad Kid feels inherently unloveable and worthless, and they expect everyone in their lives to agree with this assessment. If they do not, the Bad Kid misbehaves, hoping to get the reaction that they believe is inevitable. When people reject them as a result of this misbehavior, the Bad Kid feels validated. "See? I was right. I really am bad."

For some Bad Kids, acting out was the primary means of getting attention from their parents. To a kid, negative attention is better than no attention at all. Over time, the unwanted or "bad" behavior was reinforced, and it became a way of life.

Bad Kids often suffered emotional (and possibly other) abuse, so they have been told or shown in a variety of ways that they are bad or worthless, a lost cause, or "a mistake." When they act out and manage to drive people away, they are trapped in a vicious cycle of self-fulfilling prophecy: they believe they are bad, so they misbehave, people leave, and their belief is validated.

How the Bad Kid rules your life

If your inner child is the Bad Kid, then you sabotage your happiness daily. In relationships and on the job, you push the limits to see how much people will take before they give up on you. Those who do give up are lost opportunities—people with healthy boundaries make good friends and partners. You also risk burning bridges in your career. But there are always a handful of people who hang on and try to stick with you in spite of your attempts to push them away, but they, too, will eventually tire of having their love and loyalty for you tested at every turn. Your happiness suffers because all of your relationships suffer.

If your inner Bad Kid is *really* bad, you may have pushed it farther than just relationships and your workplace. Maybe you broke the law. Maybe you hurt someone. Maybe you hurt yourself, with drugs or alcohol. Maybe you still do.

Healing the Bad Kid

The traditional song, "The Cat Came Back" fits the Bad Kid well. In the song, Old Mister Johnson has a yellow cat that he tries to get rid of:

> *Old Mister Johnson had troubles of his own*
> *He had a yellow cat which wouldn't leave its home;*
> *He tried and he tried to give the cat away,*
> *He gave it to a man goin' far, far away.*
>
> *But the cat came back the very next day,*
> *The cat came back, we thought he was a goner*
> *But the cat came back; it just couldn't stay away.*

There are many variations of the song, but with every verse, each attempt to get rid of the cat has truly horrible consequences:

> *He gave it to a little boy with a dollar note,*
> *Told him for to take it up the river in a boat;*
> *They tied a rope around its neck, it must have weighed a pound,*
> *Now they drag the river for a little boy that's drowned.*

But the cat came back the very next day,
The cat came back, we thought he was a goner
But the cat came back; it just couldn't stay away.

He gave it to a man going up in a balloon,
He told him for to take it to the man in the moon;
The balloon came down about ninety miles away,
Where he is now, well I dare not say.

But the cat came back the very next day,
The cat came back, we thought he was a goner
But the cat came back; it just couldn't stay away.

For the Bad Kid, everyone who might care for him or her is the cat. Really, it is Love. And the Bad Kid tries very hard to make it go away so that his or her belief in their own badness will be vindicated. The solution is simple: adopt the cat! Let it into your house, feed it, pet it, and let it purr in your lap. Accept love and know that you are loveable. No one is truly bad. They are just unhealed. And healing is available to everyone, including the so-called Bad Kid.

Affirmation:

I am loved and loveable. I am the perfect me today and every day, and I forgive myself for ever doubting this.

The Perfect Kid

Also known as: The Popular Kid, The Smart Kid

The Perfect Kid never makes any mistakes. Mistakes are not allowed, but it doesn't matter, because whatever they do is perfect. If there is a risk that something might be done imperfectly, then the Perfect Kid will decline to do it, because mistakes are to the Perfect Kid what Kryptonite is to Superman: lethal.

The Perfect Kid never gets into any trouble, but they are often quick to notice when someone else has landed in trouble or done something wrong. Noticing the mistakes of others reassures the Perfect kid and reinforces the belief that *they* are on the right path.

Because the Perfect Kid is perfect, he or she suffers from the jealousy of their peers. It is hard to be friends with someone who sits on such a high pedestal, and so the Perfect Kid assumes that the other kids are too jealous to be his or her friend.

The Perfect Kid's true feelings

The Perfect Kid's greatest fear is that they are not actually perfect. Often, the Perfect Kid has parents who demand perfection and punish mistakes, so the pretense has performed an important role in the Perfect Kid's life: it has hopefully spared them from ridicule and punishment. Or maybe it hasn't. In any case, the Perfect Kid does not feel safe unless they can be perfect. The fact that this is an illusion nags at the Perfect Kid and makes them feel insecure about themselves. So when they see another kid behaving imperfectly, it is reassuring to the Perfect Kid and helps them maintain the illusion that they are better and more perfect than they actually are.

The Perfect Kid understands that the whole thing is a ruse, and their greatest fear is discovery. If someone finds out that they are not perfect, what then?

How the Perfect Kid rules your life

Perfection is a myth, but if your inner child is the Perfect Kid, then you need to believe that it is possible to be perfect. The definition of "perfect" was defined by someone other than you, however—your family of origin. Whatever they decided was perfect is how you have to live your life, even if it means living a lie. If you are living a lie to conform to someone else's definition of perfection, then you cannot find your joy. Joy comes naturally as an expression of who you really are, and if you are denying that person, then you are probably pretty miserable.

As the Perfect Kid, you fear failure to a high degree, which means you are reluctant to take risks. Your heart may tell you that you need to be an artist, or leave your partner, or be with the perfect partner, or do any number of things. But if you are afraid of what that might look like or how it might end (which you may believe is a failure in itself), then you will never open the doors that might bring you your greatest happiness.

Perfect Kids are often the product of highly critical parents, and this is a trait that you may unwittingly pass on to your children and other loved ones. When you demand perfection of yourself, you demand it of everyone around you, and no one can fulfill this expectation.

Healing the Perfect Kid

The desire to be "perfect" is really a control issue. The Perfect Kid believes in their core that there is something they "can do" or "must do" to create perfection in their lives. Failure is unthinkable, so the Perfect Kid pulls out all the stops to try to control the world around them and create perfection in their home, in their job, in their family members, and even in their community.

To heal the Perfect Kid, you must learn to release your need to control. Let a little chaos in. The world won't end. Leave the dishes until morning. Let your kid go to school without every button in place. Loosen your tie, or forget the lipstick for awhile. Take a lesson from Little Bo Peep:

Little Bo Peep has lost her sheep
And doesn't know where to find them.

Leave them alone,
And they'll come home,
Wagging their tails behind them.

Little Bo Peep, she searched for her sheep
But didn't quite know how to find them.
She looked everywhere,
From here and to there,
But still couldn't think where to find them.

Little Bo Peep began to weep
And lay down to rest for a while.
She fell fast asleep,
While counting her sheep,
Then dreamt they came home with a smile.

Little Bo Peep had fallen asleep
And dreamt that she was all alone.
But when she awoke,
And pulled back her cloak,
She saw that her sheep had come home.

Little Bo Peep had lost her sheep
And didn't know where to find them.
She left them alone,
And they came home,
Wagging their tails behind them.

When you learn to trust that your sheep will come home and the world will not fall apart without your help, then you are well on the road to a happier life that allows so-called imperfections to be what they are. Paradoxically, everything is perfect in its imperfection.

Affirmation:

There is nothing I need to do to prove my perfection. I am perfect just being who I am today and every day. I trust that everything is in divine order at all times, and there is nothing I need to do to change anything.

The Powerless Kid

Also known as: The Mean Kid, The Bully, The Shy Kid, The Loser

There are two kinds of Powerless Kids: the *aggressive* Powerless Kid and the *passive* Powerless Kid. Both feel defeated by life and are certain that there is nothing they can ever do that will be worth anything or that will make a difference to anyone. They are resigned to their own misery and wear their defeat like a badge.

The difference between them is that the aggressive Powerless Kid has gone on the offensive. Nobody's going to call *them* powerless. Instead, they're going to make everybody else feel powerless. *What are you lookin' at?* If they can demonstrate power over others, then they win.

The passive Powerless Kid, however, is happiest when they can shrink into the background; they have a lot in common with the Invisible Kid. They are pretty sure that nothing good is going to happen today, or tomorrow, or the day after that. The passive Powerless Kid feels that their life will probably suck forever, so why bother doing anything about it? They are the world's dumping ground, so everybody might as well treat them accordingly. It will never get any better. That's just the way it is, and "winning" is not in their vocabulary.

The Powerless Kid's true feelings

The aggressive Powerless Kid is also "The Mean Kid" and "The Bully." Paradoxically, bullies feel powerless, and the bullying is an attempt to feel powerful and important. They believe that controlling others will give them self-worth and erase the "I'm a loser" tape that repeats in their heads. Unfortunately, this is a short-lived fix, and no amount of power or prestige can erase these tapes because the Powerless Kid believes them in their core.

While the aggressive Powerless Kid projects their pain and feelings of worthlessness outward on the rest of the world, the passive Powerless Kid turns them inward onto his- or herself. They feel just as powerless as the aggressive version, but instead of being mean to others, they are mean to themselves. The passive Powerless Kid feels that they deserve their misery. They believe they are inherently stupid, worthless, and a general waste of space, and they believe that this can never change. They were born that way, and they will die that way. The passive Powerless Kid is frequently depressed and may suffer from a lifelong, clinical depression.

How the Powerless Kid rules your life

If your inner child is the Powerless Kid, then you cannot find joy in anything. You find it hard to believe that anyone could truly love you or want to be with you, so relationships are very difficult. There is no way that a potential partner or friend can "prove" to you that they love you or care about you, because you refuse to believe it. If your friend or partner gets frustrated by this and eventually gives up trying to convince you that they care, you say to yourself, "See? I was right. I really am unloveable."

When you believe that you are powerless, that you do not matter, and that you are inherently unloveable, then life "just happens" to you. Everything that happens to you is viewed through a dark lens, and you are a master at seeing the worst in everything. You are afraid to try something new—or make a positive change—because you "awfulize" and think of one hundred ways in which it might all backfire.

When you do not believe that you deserve anything good in life, you unconsciously make choices that ensure that nothing good will ever happen to you. It becomes a self-fulfilling prophecy.

Healing the Powerless Kid

If you believe you are powerless, it is because early in your life, your power was taken from you. You may have been emotionally abused and told that you would never amount to anything, so you decided to take control of the one thing you could and prove them right.

Your emotional life looks a great deal like this:

Humpty Dumpty sat on the wall,
Humpty Dumpty had a great fall.
All the king's horses
And all the king's men
Couldn't put Humpty Dumpty
Together again.

You became accustomed to being broken daily, and after awhile, you never bothered to pick up the pieces. Indeed, you did not think you *could* put yourself back together again, and even if you could—what was the point? Surely it was a waste of time.

Of course, this pattern of thinking—which you learned—is what robs the Powerless Kid of their power. In order to heal the Powerless Kid, you must reclaim your power and pick up those pieces of your life and your whole being. You can put yourself back together. Yes, there may be some cracks and seams—who doesn't have those? But you have the power to take an active role in your life. *You matter.* You may not believe this at first, but "fake it til you make it," as the saying goes. Begin to make new choices today. Take a risk. Consider the possibility that when someone says, "I love you," they mean it. You absolutely deserve good things and happiness, but it is up to you let them in.

Affirmation:

My thoughts and feelings are important. I stand up for what I want and need because I matter. I trust that I am loved and supported in all things.

The Chameleon

Also known as: The Popular Kid, The Class Clown

The Chameleon wants to fit in, but he or she isn't sure how to get there. But they are incredibly good at watching other people and mimicking what they do. Chameleons go with the flow, and who they are depends on who they are with. If they hang out with the jocks, they can act tough and talk football with the best of them. If they hang out with the artists, they can channel their inner Andy Warhol. If they hang out with the geeky kids, they can wax rhapsodic about technology. Whatever the situation, a Chameleon knows how to blend in. They are consummate actors.

The Chameleon's true feelings

The Chameleon's desire to blend in with their surroundings is based on their need to be accepted and validated by others. The worst thing that can happen to a Chameleon is for someone to reject them, because the Chameleon believes that this is a judgment of their worth. This fear of rejection may be rooted in a very real and painful rejection in their past, possibly by a parent (who may have left the family, divorced, etc.) or another important figure.

Chameleons secretly lack confidence in their ability to make and keep friends. They do not believe that who they really are is enough to make anyone like them, so they create a variety of masks that they wear for different occasions so that others will like or approve of them.

How the Chameleon rules your life

The problem with continually wearing masks and acting a part is that you start to forget who you really are. The longer you do it, the more "lost" the real you becomes. As a result, you become accustomed to living for everyone but yourself. You no longer know what *you* really want or don't want. Instead, you are constantly "scanning" the situation to find out what others want *from* you. You live an inauthentic existence, and no one can truly be happy unless they live authentically.

Unfortunately, after all those years of acting a part, you have forgotten what your authentic self looks like. Figuring out who you are and what you really want or need for yourself can seem like an impossible task, like digging for buried treasure.

Healing the Chameleon

The Chameleon is so good at absorbing the wants and needs of others (and repressing their own) that they are like the little teapot in the song:

I'm a little teapot, short and stout;
Here is my handle, here is my spout.
When I get all steamed up, hear me shout,
Just tip me over and pour me out!

I'm a clever teapot, yes it's true;
Here's an example of what I can do.
I can change my handle to my spout.
Just tip me over and pour me out!

Like the teapot, the Chameleon gets filled up with the expectations of everyone around them. When they are no longer needed, the Chameleon pours them out and gets filled up again.

To heal this, the Chameleon must embark on a voyage of self-discovery. Who are you when no one is in the room? What does that person need and want? What desires, activities, interests, or career possibilities were pushed aside because you were afraid someone would not approve? If you were given one month to live, how would you most want to spend that time?

As you get to know yourself, you must simultaneously work to accept that person. You are enough, right now, in this very moment, just as you are. Your happiness is not dependent on pleasing others; it is dependent on pleasing *you*. If someone does not like who you really are, then you are better off without them. There are countless people out there who *will* like and accept you as you are, but unless you can *be* that person, then how will you know? How will anyone else ever know you if you do not give them the chance?

Affirmation:

I am enough, just as I am. I honor and embrace my wants, needs, interests, and talents. I love my authentic self, and I trust that others will, too.

The Outsider

Also known as: The Poor Kid, The Misfit, The Rebel

The Outsider does not belong anywhere, lives outside the mainstream, and is the ultimate nonconformist—a badge that the Outsider wears with pride. No one understands them, and no one ever will, so the Outsider becomes a martyr to the loneliness and isolation that is apparently their destiny. "Screw society," says the Outsider. "I don't need it anyway."

The Outsider's true feelings

The truth is that the Outsider *does* need society, and their worst nightmare is to be cast adrift in it, all alone, neither loving nor being loved. It is human nature to want to connect and to be understood, to be appreciated and accepted. On the outside, the Outsider may appear to scorn society's seeming rejection of them, but the truth is that it hurts them a lot on the inside. The Outsider may grieve this rejection, leading to depression. Or, in true rebel style, it may give way to outwardly directed anger.

How the Outsider rules your life

If your inner child feels like an Outsider, then avoiding rejection is a big priority for you. If you have been at it for long enough, then you expect to be rejected in any social situation. Because this is so painful, your inner child has probably decided that he or she will do the rejecting *first*. When this happens, no person is ever allowed to become truly close to you, whether as a friend or a romantic partner. If a person starts to get too close—if they begin to see the real you beneath your protective armor—you find a way to sabotage the relationship and make them go away. And when they do leave your life, you say to yourself, "Aha! Rejected yet again. I knew I was right not to trust them. I'll always be an Outsider." And so you create a self-fulfilling prophecy. You remain lonely, unhappy, and misunderstood.

Healing the Outsider

The Outsider feels deeply unloved by everyone around them, but this is a reflection of how they feel about themselves: that they are unloveable. Feeling unloveable and believing their own imagined bad press, the Outsider believes that they are unworthy of the company of "good, normal people." This being the case, the Outsider is convinced that they do not deserve anything good:

Nobody likes me, everybody hates me,
I think I'll go eat worms!
Big fat juicy ones,
Eensie weensy squeensy ones,
See how they wiggle and squirm!

Down goes the first one, down goes the second one,
Oh how they wiggle and squirm!
Up comes the first one, up comes the second one,
Oh how they wiggle and squirm!

I bite off the heads, and suck out the juice,
And throw the skins away!
Nobody knows how fat I grow,
On worms three times a day!

Nobody likes me, everybody hates me,
I think I'll go eat worms!
Big fat juicy ones,
Eensie weensy squeensy ones,
See how they wiggle and squirm!

Everyone encounters rejection in their life, and some people are not going to like you. Even more unfortunately, sometimes the people who do not seem to approve of you are family members who, in theory, are supposed to love you and support you. The tragedy is when the inner child grows up with very little external approval at all, which they then internalize and come to believe that, yes, they really must be as awful as people say. The fact that this is not true does not deter the inner child from believing it.

As your grown-up self, however, you now have the opportunity to affirm your own value for yourself. You do not deserve to eat worms every day. You *do* deserve to be happy and live a joyful life. It may take some time and patience to convince your inner child of this fact, but start by believing that it is the truth, because it is.

When you start to affirm your own value to yourself, you will discover an interesting thing: other people will begin to affirm your worthiness as well. Not everyone will. But the *right people* will. Eventually, you will discover that you can create your own community of like-minded people, and you will cease to be an Outsider.

Affirmation:

My value is not dependent on the judgments of others. I value myself and know my own worth. I deserve love and companionship, and I now have the perfect companions for me.

Which archetype is in control?

Once you have identified some of the archetypes that apply to you, you can use them as a tool. If something is not working for you, or if a situation or interaction keeps repeating with results that you do not like, ask yourself what archetype may be at work in that situation. What are you feeling? Certain feelings habitually lead to certain reactions in yourself. If you can identify the feeling, then you can understand the cause of the reaction. What is your inner child telling you when this occurs?

When you have answers to these questions, you can begin to make new choices. If your fear of rejection leads you to an outcome that you do not like, then respond to your inner child with an affirmation of some kind, or simply reassure them. "The right people will not reject you. I do not reject myself." This will undoubtedly feel uncomfortable or forced at first, but over time, your new choices will lead you to success.

Your parents and other false gods

Every people have gods to suit their circumstances.
—Henry David Thoreau

All children learn that the authority figures in their life call the shots. Hopefully, these authority figures met your needs: they loved and cherished you, respected you, gave you boundaries, kept you safe, and kept you clothed, fed, and sheltered. It is likely, however, that your authority figures failed you in some ways, as well.

From your inner child's perspective, the authority figures in your life were and are gods. As such, you subconsciously believe that they are infallible, and any secret doubt that you may have about their infallibility is considered to be high treason—by you as well as others.

By believing that the power of your gods is absolute and that you cannot question their influence, you ensure that your needs continue to go unmet and prevent yourself from healing from the past. Your gods must be unmasked—not to dishonor them or disrespect their role in your life—but instead to see them as they truly are and loosen their grip on your life.

Your inner child's gods come in many forms, and they will continue to control your life until you decide to remove them from their pedestal, where *you* placed them, and take back the power you let them have over you.

Your inner child's gods

Just about anything can be an authority figure in your life. Some authority figures are appropriate: a parent, a teacher, a boss, or a doctor. Some authority figures, however, can be inappropriate, including a parent, teacher, boss, or doctor. What is the difference?

When we decide, often subconsciously, that someone is an authority figure, we are giving them power over us. We are effectively saying that the authority figure knows better than we do in some circumstances, and we defer to their knowledge and wishes. You can't know everything, and deferring to your doctor's trained opinion is usually a good idea—except when it isn't. How do you know?

We all have a "gut instinct" or an inner knowing that guides us. Spirit talks to us in this way. Sometimes, you "just know" what you need to do. Whether or not you act on that depends on how willing you are to let others talk you out of it, or how willing you are to let the opinions of others sway you. This is when authority figures become gods and control your life.

Human gods

A wise person will listen to and consider the counsel of others, but ultimately, they will decide for themselves. A person who is ruled by gods allows the gods to decide for them.

No one knows what you need and what you should do better than you do. No one knows *you* better than you do, not even your parents, spouse, or best friend. In healthy relationships, your loved ones will not ask you to deny what you know to be true in yourself. They may caution, advise, and worry, but they will not use their influence over you to urge you to do something that is out of integrity with who you are. There is no need for gods in healthy relationships.

Not all relationships are healthy, however, and not all people behave with integrity. If you were taught as a child to respect the absolute authority of someone who acted disrespectfully, unkindly, or even abusively, then this pattern is probably alive and well in your life today. You give away your power unconsciously to people who do not deserve it or who abuse it. As a result, you may experience unhappy, abusive, or unequal relationships in which you allow others to decide how your life will be.

The problem with gods is that their presumed infallibility means that you cannot question their authority. And if you cannot question their authority, you have to come up with reasons why it is okay to let them treat you badly. Your inner child began this process to try to make sense of the world: if a god was treating you badly, your inner child decided that you must deserve it. And the only thing that your child self could think to do was submit to it.

You do not have to submit to it, of course. As an adult, you can see that and know that, but your inner child is your emotional core, and he or she needs some convincing. That is what this work is all about.

You *can* reclaim your power, assert your boundaries, and retake your role as the primary decision maker in your life. In order to do that, you must unmask your gods.

Other gods

People are not the only gods that we place on the altar of our life. Anything has the power to become a god and take control, including:

- Money (the desire or need for more, or the fear of not having enough)
- Drugs or alcohol

- Food

- Sex

- Work

- Security

- Time

- Fear of failure

- Fear of anything

- The need to be "right"

- The need to look or act "right"

- Obsessions of any kind

Whenever we decide that something is more important than our own well being, or the well being of our loved ones, we have created a god.

Some of the things in this list are not necessarily a problem in themselves. Money is not a problem or a "bad" thing—unless the desire to gain it or the fear of not having enough of it rules your life. Money can become very tightly wound in your ego and in your emotional body. Not having enough money can make you feel like a colossal failure or provide you with more ammunition to beat yourself up. This is a replay of "I deserve not to have any, and I am not worthy," which you learned as a child. On the other hand, if you amass a fortune, your inner child may feel that it is finally worth something—even if the price of that fortune is your happiness or relationships.

Again, in this example, money itself is not the problem, but giving it the power to validate our own worth as a human being is. When money is our god, we think, "I will be happy when I have a million dollars," or "I will be happy when I pay off this credit card." If you are not happy now, no matter what your finances are, having money will not change things.

Almost anything can become an addiction as well, and when that happens, it clearly has control of your life. In truth, your inner child turns to its various gods in an attempt to find validation—that you are loveable, that you are "good," that you are worthy. And like most children do, if your inner child is not receiving what they need, they act out and try to get the gods' attention by doing "bad" things.

Parents

I saw my parents as gods whose every wish must be
obeyed, or I would suffer the penalty of anguish and guilt.
—Natalie Wood

Your parents play a huge role in the world of your inner child, even if you never knew them. They are gods by default, because they had tremendous power over you as a child, and that influence continues—for better or worse—through today.

Your parents helped shape who you are, and they helped define your inner child's mental, emotional, and spiritual landscape. Even if you disagree with your parents on practically every point, your inner child cannot escape the impact that they had on you.

For the inner child, the term "parents" may include the following people:

- Biological parents

- Step-parents

- Adopted parents

- Foster parents

- Deceased or absent parents

- Grandparents

- Other guardians (aunt, uncle, etc.)

You may have had any combination of parents, and even if they were dead or absent, they had an effect on you. An absent parent can be a formidable god, because your inner child has more freedom to imagine the best—or worst—about them. A deceased parent, on the other hand, can become even more godlike because your inner child is afraid that reducing them to mere human status will dishonor their memory.

Benevolent parents

The world is full of great, loving parents. Benevolent parents show their children with their words and actions that they are loved and respected. In all likelihood, this is done imperfectly; parents are human beings who make mistakes. Nevertheless, the child receives the message that they are loved and valued.

If you were lucky enough to have at least one really good parent, you may tend to believe that your inner child has no issues, but that probably is not true. Every inner child has feelings and beliefs based on their upbringing, and even seemingly benign parental behaviors can negatively impact your inner child. In fact, if you had good parents, it can be *even harder* to recognize and deal with your inner child's issues because you feel that naming these issues is somehow a betrayal of the people you love dearly.

It is important to understand that your inner child's feelings are just that: feelings. They may not seem logical to your adult mind. They may not even make sense at first. If you discover that you are carrying some anger at your "good" parents, your first instinct will be to deny your own anger, because why on earth would these loving people make your inner child angry? It can't be something about them, so it must be your failure for feeling that way. You must be "wrong" for feeling that way.

Anger and grief are common inner child emotions, but since people tend to view them as "negative," they tend to believe that they cannot hold these emotions about their parents and love them at the same time. But of course, you can feel angry with your parents about something and still love them. You can feel grief at not getting quite what you needed from them and still love them. Even good parents make mistakes and have inner child issues themselves.

Benevolent parents are particularly potent gods because of the fear that removing the mask of their godhood will reveal imperfect people—and it will. Everyone is an imperfect person who is doing the best that they can. The challenge you face in growing up and reclaiming yourself is to see your parents not as powerful gods, but as people.

Your parents should become your special friends and peers—your equal. When you can make this shift, you gain a fulfilling relationship in which you can interact with your parents as your grown-up self instead of feeling like you are six years old every time you go home again.

Toxic parents

Simply having children does not make mothers.
—John A. Shedd

No parent is perfect, and even "good" parents may exhibit a few toxic behaviors that your inner child must deal with. Some parents, however, are very toxic and leave a legacy of abuse behind them. If your inner child does not heal this, it is very likely that you will repeat some of the same patterns that your parents taught you.

If you have a toxic parent, you might have a love-hate relationship with them. You may love them because they are your parent, but you may also really hate their behavior. And if the behavior was bad enough, you may not love them at all.

Whether you love or hate your parent, or fall somewhere in between, they are a god in your life. Consider this: when someone makes you angry, you are giving them power over you. Your anger ultimately hurts you, not your parents. This is why it is so important to help your inner child release this powerful emotion.

What is a toxic parent?

A toxic parent fails to meet the physical, mental, emotional, or spiritual needs of their children in some way. They also fail to provide a safe environment for their children. This can mean that the child is physically abused or neglected—their basic needs are not met, they are not adequately supervised or disciplined; children who "run wild" are as neglected as those who are micro-managed. An unsafe environment, however, can also mean that the child is mentally, emotionally, or spiritually unsafe in the home.

If a child does not feel free to express themselves, if they must "hide" themselves, if they fear ridicule or humiliation, if they can never measure up or please the parent, then they are emotionally and mentally unsafe in their own home. This is a classic by-product of a toxic parent.

By contrast, a benevolent parent is one who may mistakes, but who looks after the physical, emotional, mental, and spiritual needs of their children. A benevolent parent praises a child and provides constructive feedback. A benevolent parent does not attempt to "tear down" their child in order to make themselves feel better. A benevolent parent understands the importance of structure and boundaries. A toxic parent is rarely capable of providing either of these.

Of course, a toxic parent can appear to be very loving— even downright needy. But in this kind of relationship, the toxic parent assumes the role of the child and expects the child to fulfill all their needs. The child can't accomplish this, so they feel like a failure. "Needy" parents who expect validation from their children, or who expect their children to "take care" of them or make them happy, are just as toxic as those who are more outwardly abusive.

Parents who are neglectful and overly passive are also toxic parents. An ignored child is an abused child. And the parent who stands by while another parent abuses the child is a partner in the abuse.

Types of toxic parents

There are all types of toxic parents, more than I could possibly include in this book, but in general they look like everybody else. From the outside, they may appear to be model parents. Inside the home, however, things are not "all right."

Toxic parents were often abused as children, and in some cases, the parent may actually be mentally ill, but undiagnosed. The toxic parent may suffer from any of the following illnesses or disorders:[1]

Alcoholism

Addictions become gods in themselves, and they become the primary goal and focus of the addict. Everything else is secondary—including children. An alcoholic's toxic behavior (an easily triggered temper, low self-esteem, hurtful behavior, a need to be constantly validated), can occur with people who no longer drink or who drink very little or not at all, however. This is called

---

[1] Some of these disorders are described in the American Psychiatric Association's *Diagnostic and Statistical Manual of Mental Disorders IV.* The naming and classification of these disorders may change with the release of *Diagnostic and Statistical Manual of Mental Disorders V.* However, regardless of the label that is used, the behaviors that are described have a significant impact on the inner child.

dry drunk behavior, and it is a pattern of coping that is often learned by the child of an alcoholic parent.

Drug addiction (illegal or prescription)

Toxic behavior from a drug addict is very similar to an alcoholic's. It is also not unusual for an addicted parent to try to offload their guilt onto their children by encouraging them to become addicts as well. Children of addicts are at a high risk for becoming addicted themselves.

Depression

Depression is crippling. A clinically depressed person can barely hold it together to take care of themselves, much less a child. Depressed people have trouble meeting basic needs, sleep a lot, have suicidal thoughts, and are generally apathetic toward the world. Fortunately, treatment is available, but the burden typically falls to the depressed person to seek it out.

Antisocial Personality Disorder

Also known as sociopaths or psychopaths, these people are extremely abusive and can be dangerous. On the outside, however, they often appear to be very charming, attractive, intelligent, and successful. They often rise to positions of power and prestige. And yet, they have no sense of compassion or caring for others and only seek to fulfill their own needs or wishes—even at the expense of others. If they feel that someone has "crossed" them or is interfering with their wants or needs, they may "go cold" and frighten the person they feel has crossed them. If you cross a person with this disorder, they typically seek retribution and will make you pay for it when they find the perfect opportunity.

Bipolar Disorder

People with Bipolar Disorder suffer from extreme mood swings, and in the past this was called Manic-Depressive Disorder. Without treatment, a person who suffers from Bipolar Disorder may experience giddy highs when they are full of energy and ready to cheerfully take on the world. Yet, an ocean of anger may lie beneath this cheerful mask, and it can flare up instantly if the person feels crossed. After the "high" period comes a period of dark depression that is immobilizing. People with this disorder can display very erratic behaviors that can be damaging to a child. They are not in control of their reactions to the world, and even with the help of medication, they may still battle mood swings.

Borderline Personality Disorder (BPD)

People with BPD do not have a strong sense of self. As a result, they often take on the characteristics of the people they are around, sort of like "human chameleons"—they adapt themselves to mirror the personalities of the people in the room. People with BPD are frequently intelligent and distinguish themselves in their chosen careers, but in their interpersonal relationships, they experience extreme shifts in moods and have a hard time controlling the expression of their feelings. For example, they may express their anger in ways that most people would consider to be extreme: screaming, using foul language, saying hurtful things. And when they are happy, they are very, very happy. When the emotional weather changes from sunny high noon to darkest night at the drop of a hat, it's very confusing and damaging to a young child. Children with a borderline parent may blame themselves for their parent's unpredictable moods.

Histrionic Personality Disorder

People with this disorder crave attention, and they bring it to themselves by being overly dramatic and "stirring the pot" to create conflict. A peaceful, loving environment is not their goal. At its worst, histrionics will manipulate the people they love to create problems where none existed before, allowing them to be "the hero" amid the chaos they have created.

Obsessive-compulsive Disorder

People with this disorder have strange, compulsive behaviors that they must do to perfection. For example, a person may have a need to straighten all the pictures in a room when they enter it. Howard Hughes famously suffered from this, and he washed his hands so frequently that they bled. These compulsions are a cover for extreme anxieties, and performing these actions soothes the person with the disorder and helps keep them sane. Medication may help this disorder.

Obsessive-compulsive Personality Disorder (OCPD)

People with OCPD are perfectionists and workaholics who are often highly educated and have prestigious careers. The need to be perfect is a crippling disease. This issue inevitably makes its way into The Family Myth, in which the whole family is required to be seen as "perfect" and "keep up" with the person who has this disorder. No one can live up to such high expectations, so children of people with OCPD may feel like failures or refuse to try new things or take risks for fear of failing. Some children may come to believe wholeheartedly in The Family Myth and therefore have a hard time seeing and understanding their own or their family's shortcomings. Unfortunately, this trait is all too easily passed from one generation to the next. Sometimes OCPD is a symptom of another disorder, such as Narcissistic Personality Disorder.

Narcissistic Personality Disorder (NPD)

Narcissists lack compassion and empathy. They are critical and contemptuous of others, lack a sense of humor, cannot recognize their true feelings, have a poor memory, are competitive, and contradict themselves often. They live in a fantasy world in which they have absolute power, beauty, and genius, which they expect everyone to recognize. Your memory of events and the narcissist's memory will seldom match, because the narcissist has already rewritten events in their head in order to see themselves in a better light. Narcissists will be your best friend if you agree with their fantasies about themselves, but failing to validate them (by disagreeing with them) brings swift retribution. They are very quick to stab you in the back. Children of narcissists grow up believing that everything that is wrong in the relationship is due to their own failure—never the narcissist's. Often, children of narcissists either come to believe in the narcissist's fantasy, or they see the truth and disagree, making them the target of the narcissist's wrath. Narcissists are emotionally and verbally abusive, and sometimes resort to physical abuse as well.

Rageaholism

Rage makes children (and adults) feel completely unsafe. When a parent's rage is directed at you as a child, your whole world feels dangerous. And when you never know when the volcano will erupt, you are walking on eggshells all of your life. Children of rageaholics often learn to "fly under the radar" so that they don't get noticed, which decreases their chances of being the target of a rage. Such "survival mode" skills see the child through to adulthood, but they can get in the way of goals and dreams later.

Don't let the psychological labels fool you. Don't think your parent could have a psychological diagnosis? If you have a toxic parent, think again. We do not want to see our parents as imperfect, but they are, whether they are diagnosable or not, or whether they are toxic or not. If your parent does have a disorder or addiction of some kind, it can be helpful for your healing to recognize it, and one or more of these labels may apply. The knowledge that your parent's behavior is *not* normal helps to take the burden off of your shoulders and put it where it belongs: on theirs.

That being said, none of these labels may apply, and you may still have a toxic parent. Just having very low self-esteem is generally enough to produce some toxic behavior. Also, many individuals may have traits of any of the disorders described previously without actually having the disorder itself. For example, a person may not have full-blown Narcissistic Personality Disorder, but they may have strong traits of the disorder. When any of these patterns of toxic behavior are expressed continuously by parents or caregivers, it creates a very difficult (or abusive) environment for children to grow up in.

Is your parent toxic?

In general, if you answer "yes" to one or more of these, you may have toxic parents:

- Do you often feel frustrated after talking to your parents?

- Do you often feel angry with your parents, even if you're not sure why?

- After interacting with your parents, do you often feel worse about yourself?

- Do you feel unheard by your parents?

- Do you feel like your parents don't care about your feelings?

- Do you feel "punished" for having a different opinion than your parents do?

- Do your parents punish you by withdrawing their love?

- Do your parents frequently criticize you or make fun of you?

- Do your parents use derogatory language when they talk about you (i.e., call you stupid, dumb, ugly, etc.)?

- Do your parents often excuse their actions by blaming you for them, or by saying that they are only doing things for your own good?

- Do your parents try to control your life, even though you are an adult?

- Do you feel that your parents dislike you?

If you have toxic parents, you have toxic gods. From your inner child's perspective, the ultimate authority in your universe does not seem to approve of you or even like you very much. That is tremendously damaging to a child's mind and self-esteem.

Of course, if you have toxic parent gods, then God with a capital "G" is probably toxic as well.

When God is a toxic parent

Men create the gods in their own image.
—Xenophanes

When people turn away from religion, it is often because they have been spiritually abused by a representation of God who is a harsh, vengeful, uncompromising father figure who will punish them for eternity if they step out of line—a line drawn, conveniently, by others. People who have experienced such a God may reject all spirituality, and just mentioning the word "God" can cause them to run far, far away.

No soul should be oppressed, particularly by a definition of God, and every soul instinctively wants to express what it is and how it is, no matter what that looks like. But if you believe in a God who is a toxic, judgmental parent, you are living in fear. You are afraid to offend "him" and you are afraid of losing "his" love by your thoughts, feelings, and actions. When you live in fear, you hide your true self. You hate your true self. You are convinced of your inherent "badness."

Like a toxic parent, a toxic god fails to meet the physical, mental, or emotional needs of their children in some way. A person who is convinced that God's love could turn to hate and rejection on the basis of who they are, how they feel, and what they do is mentally, emotionally, and spiritually abused. When God is a toxic parent, it can crush you.

Being raised by real, physical toxic parents is difficult enough and requires a lot of healing in some cases. But when the ultimate authority in the Universe—the being who created you—is portrayed as a toxic parent, what hope do you have? How can you ever gain such a figure's approval? How can you ever be good? How can you ever be loveable, imperfections and all? The answer is: you can't. So the children of a toxic god either run away and leave this "spiritual home" behind, or they continue to live in fear and believe in their own inherent worthlessness.

We all have our own view of what God (or Spirit) is, but when you create a personality for God, you do two things: first, you declare that God is separate from yourself, and second, you project your own ego onto God, effectively making God in your own image. When this happens, God takes on the complex, contradictory qualities that you embody. For example, the God of love becomes capable of hate. The God of forgiveness becomes capable of vengeance and holding a grudge. God becomes arbitrary, unhealed, and a slave to "his" perceived emotions, becoming angry at you and threatening to send you to your room if you do not think or behave the "right" way. In short, this God acts a lot like a toxic parent—even an addicted parent.

The psychological impact of having God as a toxic parent in your life is profound. Your ability to be gentle with yourself, love yourself, and be happy depends on healing this relationship and knowing, for yourself, that God would never treat you this way. However, *you* treat yourself this way if you accept this view of God. Ultimately, *you* must decide if you are worthy, loveable, and precious, and you must stop using God as an excuse to beat yourself up. God will not punish you, but *you* can.

Certainly, there are people in the world who act as enablers for God the toxic parent. When God reflects our own ego back to us, it feels like a validation. Some people want that badly, but it is not enough for them to have it for themselves. They want you to validate them, too. If you subscribe to their vision of God, they feel empowered. But God has no favorites and needs no further empowering. God is the perfect parent, male and female. God is unconditional love. God is forgiveness. God is the sweet embrace of eternity and joy and complete unity, because there is no separation between us and God (or Spirit) at all.

6

Recognizing abuse and toxic patterns

Children are like wet cement. Whatever falls on them makes an impression.
—Dr. Haim Ginott

When you have lived a certain way your entire life and your personal interactions with others have always followed a specific script, then it feels normal to you. This is the way the world works; this is the way that people behave. It can be hard to imagine an alternative way to be. This is all you know.

But the way relationships work in your family is not the way they work in all families. Some families have healthier ways of relating to one another, and some families have more toxic ways. Most families fall somewhere in the middle, exhibiting both healthy and toxic patterns. The challenge for you as an adult is to learn to distinguish which is which, so that you can help your inner child to heal and make healthier choices.

Human beings are complex, and there are more possible behaviors in existence than can be included in this book, but the following descriptions are meant to help you to understand what kinds of behavior are harmful and oppressive.

What is abuse?

When someone was hitting me, or like sexually molesting me, it just seemed normal to continue to do that to myself.
—Tatum O'Neal

Abusive people are toxic people, and they seldom recognize when they are being abusive. They are simply repeating the patterns that their inner child learned, and for many, their behavior is "just how people do things." Toxic people were often abused themselves, and they grew up believing that they deserved the abuse. In some cases, of course, the abuser is mentally ill.

If you were abused in any way as a child, there was no rational thought process that helped you to understand that it was happening because of your parents' own inner child issues or mental illness. Abuse was arbitrary, mysterious, uncontrollable, and a part of your landscape. It is what "normal" felt like. Nevertheless, it is human nature to try to understand why things happen. Since abuse is not rational, your inner child likely decided that it was happening to you because you did something to deserve it. As a result, you probably internalized some shame, as well, as though you were to blame for what happened to you.

When most people think about what abuse is, they tend to think of actions that cause someone physical pain: slapping, punching, burning, pinching, or physically torturing others in any way. While this kind of abuse is truly horrible, it is not the only way that people abuse others. As a result, you may have grown up being abused without even realizing it.

Physical abuse

Physical abuse comes in many forms. Sometimes, it is severe, and people are badly tortured or even killed by it. Sometimes, however, it is more subtle. Physical punishment is abuse, too, particularly if it was applied with a belt or tree limb or even a hot cigarette on your skin. If you were physically hurt in any way (particularly if it was done as a "punishment"), then you were abused.

Physical abuse may include (but is not limited to) the following:

- Hitting
- Slapping
- Spanking
- Pushing
- Jerking by the arm
- Burning
- Dunking in water

Sexual abuse

Like physical abuse, sexual abuse is a very obvious form of abuse. There is rarely any question that children who suffer this are abused. Nevertheless, the family narrative may seek to put the blame for it on the victim—on the child—instead of the perpetrator, where it belongs. When this happens, the parents— whether they committed the crime or simply remained passive while it occurred—are unconsciously attempting to place *their* guilt on the child. The child readily accepts the blame, not knowing any better and endeavoring to please or placate the parents.

Any sexual contact or play (including excessive tickling) that is forced on a child by an adult is abuse. Showing pornography of any kind to a child is also abuse.

Emotional abuse

In many ways, emotional abuse is the most difficult because it is so easy to overlook. It leaves no physical scars, so it is not obvious to an onlooker that there is a problem in the family. Children who are emotionally abused also may not be aware that this is what is happening; to them, it is just how the world works. Some children gain an awareness that their environment is not healthy—it is not how the world is supposed to be—fairly early in life. And some children grow up before they understand this, while some may never realize how they were abused.

Emotional abuse may include (but is not limited to) the following:

- Calling you demeaning names

- Using demeaning language, such as "Are you too stupid to figure this out?"

- Constantly criticizing

- Belittling

- Being dismissive of your wants, needs, or concerns

- Excessive teasing or making fun of you

- Constantly comparing you to others in a negative way

- Always assuming that you are lying, untrustworthy, or incompetent

- Using you to "get back" at the other parent

- Setting you up to fail

- Having unreasonable expectations

- Disrespecting your person, your property, or your boundaries

- Making you feel guilty for your choices

- Using emotional blackmail to get you to do what they want

- Consistently doing the opposite of what you want or need—being passive-aggressive

- Engaging in behaviors that make you feel unsafe

- Just being mean

- Consistently hurting your feelings or making you feel bad about yourself in any way

One of the most difficult aspects of emotional abuse is that the parent may have the capacity for nearly infinite deniability. If you were physically abused, no one could dispute the physical evidence of that—you feel physical pain and have the bruises or scars to show for it. But with emotional abuse, the abuser may excuse themselves with a wide variety of arguments, leaving you to doubt your own mind and feelings. Some abusers are so skilled at deflecting blame for their abuse, that you may convince yourself that *you* are the one with the problem because you feel angry and hurt by what has happened to you. This is particularly a problem when the abusive parent is still a false god—your ultimate authority figure. So they must be right. Right?

Parents who try to deflect the blame for their emotional abuse may say things like:

- I'm not criticizing you; I'm trying to help you.

- It's your own fault.

- You're making a mountain out of a molehill.

- You're too sensitive.

- Get over it.

- You just have to accept me the way I am.

What these statements all have in common is that ultimately, if you are upset, then it is *your* fault—not your parent's. Unfortunately, your inner child got this message loud and clear and believes it, even if you now know better.

Neglect

Neglect is also a form of abuse, but unlike the kinds listed above (which are *active*), neglect is *passive*. If you were neglected, no one took care of your needs: physical, emotional, or spiritual.

Neglect may include (but is not limited to) the following:

- Failing to provide food, clothing, or adequate shelter

- Inability to adhere to a routine or schedule

- Consistent tardiness or missing deadlines

- Failure or inability to meet your emotional needs

- Lack of physical warmth (hugs, cuddles, etc.)

- Consistently being unaware of where you were and failing to find you or ask where you were

- Consistently fulfilling their own needs before attending to yours

- Standing by (doing nothing) while other kinds of abuse occur

An addicted parent may be abusive (physically, sexually, or emotionally), but they are also frequently neglectful as well, failing to ensure that you had enough to eat, adhered to a schedule, got where you needed to be, etc. Likewise, the parent who stands by while another parent actively abuses children is a neglectful parent and a partner in the abuse.

Common toxic patterns

Most human beings have at least a few toxic patterns that they have inherited, even if they had super parents, but very often people are unaware of them. You may frequently find yourself involved in certain toxic "loops" with one or more family members, which leaves you feeling frustrated and unhappy. For example, you may continually have the same argument or misunderstanding. At the end of it, you feel unheard, misunderstood, and possibly unloved because of your thoughts, beliefs, or actions. Why does this keep happening?

A toxic "loop" is simply a pattern that happens over and over again, and because it happens so frequently, it becomes "comfortable" and familiar, even if it makes you unhappy. You know what it feels like. You do X; they say Y, and you are pulled like metal to a magnet back into the old disagreement. You feel like you are defending yourself; they feel the same way. Who wins? The answer is: no one ever does.

The fact that no one really wins does not prevent people from trying. In the battle to "win" or be "right," people will often stop at nothing, because the alternative according to *their* inner child is to lose, be "wrong," or be rejected. And if their inner child is very afraid of this outcome, he or she will keep at it, even if it means hurting someone else. Even if it means hurting you.

The following toxic behaviors are extremely common—so much so that many people think of them as normal. But seeing a thing for what it is—toxic—is the first step in being able to deal with it in a healthy way, and to heal it in yourself, as well.

Criticism

Thoughtful criticism has its place, and many people are open to it in the form of *constructive feedback*. Constructive feedback points out strengths as well as any weaknesses, and it is offered kindly, often with suggestions for improvement. We all need constructive feedback, and we can recognize it because the result is that we continue to feel good about ourselves and about the person who is giving the feedback.

Criticism, on the other hand, feels very different. Our feelings are hurt, and we become unhappy with the person delivering it. If the critic remains unapologetic about this state of affairs, then more hurt follows.

Over time, criticism can erode self-esteem. Bullies always criticize and say hurtful things to their victims, and it is very common for the victim to come to doubt their sense of self-worth as a result. In so doing, the victim remains a victim and hands *their* power over to the bully. In this scenario, the bully wins and manages to feel slightly better about themselves for five minutes.

Anyone who constantly criticizes others is a bully, and what they are really trying to do is to inflate their own low sense of self-worth. It is important to recognize this behavior for what it is, so that you do not get sucked into the cycle of doubting your own sense of worth as a result.

Gaslighting

Gaslighting is similar to criticism, except that it goes on for an extended time with the purpose of making you doubt yourself or believe something false about yourself, which makes it easier for the person doing it to control you. Sometimes gaslighting is premeditated and done with malicious intent. Sometimes gaslighting is done unconsciously, with the unstated goal of exerting control over another and building up a fragile ego.

The term itself comes from the classic film, *Gaslight*, with Ingrid Bergman. In the film, she portrays a woman who has married a toxic, criminal man who isolates her and works to convince her in various ways that she is going mad. In the plot, he never really wants *her*, but rather the fortune hidden in the house that she has inherited.

When someone tries to gaslight another person, they deny and lie, often convincingly, in order to make their victim doubt their own experience, feelings, and perception. For the gaslighter, this is their method of gaining control over another person, which becomes easier as their intended victim loses confidence and doubts their own mind. Spouses or partners who are emotionally or physically abusive often gaslight their victims in order to prevent them from leaving or seeking help.

Passive-aggressive behavior

Passive-aggressive behavior is actually an expression of anger, except no yelling or arguing is involved. Instead, the passive-aggressive person gives the *appearance* of agreeing with what you say or what your stated goals are, but then they passively undermine you by consistently doing the *opposite* of what you want or thought you both had agreed upon.

Passive-aggressive behavior is the perfect mask for "stealth anger." It is so effective that passive-aggressive people often believe—even insist—that they are not angry. They do not see their behavior for what it is and are typically unaware that they are doing it.

The heart of passive aggression is the desire to thwart others. The inner child seems to think, "You think you can control me, but *I'll* show you." Nothing is ever said, but the passive-aggressive person simply fails to do what they agreed to do, refuses to play by the rules, and goes out of their way to hold up others.

Do you know someone who is chronically late? Being consistently late is a form of passive aggression. Do they make a big scene when they finally arrive, diverting attention to themselves (and away from someone else)?

The object of the passive-aggressive person is to gain control of any situation. If their spouse says, "Honey, could you wash the dishes?" they may reply with, "Yes," but then they may let them sit until their spouse gives up and does them anyway. When a passive-aggressive person is late for a meeting, appointment, holiday dinner, etc., they are trying to take control of every other person in the room by making them wait.

In another example from the newspaper column "Ask Amy," a woman was dealing with a mother-in-law who gave her a Christmas list every year that described all of the things she *did not* want to receive. The daughter-in-law shopped carefully and dutifully bought her something that was not on the list, only to have this gift appear on the "do not buy" list the following year. This is textbook passive-aggressive behavior.

Emotional blackmail

At the heart of all toxic behavior is the desire to control and manipulate others into validating one's own beliefs and opinions, to have others behave in a certain way, or simply to gain attention. And the Ace card in the toxic manipulator's deck is emotional blackmail.

Unfortunately, the people who are most likely to use this tool on you are the ones you love the most, because they expect that you will care enough about them to do whatever it is *they* want—even if it is the opposite of what you want or are comfortable with. A casual acquaintance cannot have this kind of hold on you, so even if they did try to use it, you are more likely to stand firm and do what is right for you and your conscience.

The emotional blackmailer seeks to make *you* solely responsible for all of their problems. If they are unhappy, it is *your* fault. If they are poor, it is *your* fault. If they are ill, it is *your* fault. If they are suicidal, it is definitely *your* fault. Their only pathway to happiness and a decent life, it would seem, lies through *you*.

This is neither true nor fair, of course. If one person expects a second person to take on the burden of their entire life and happiness, it must surely mean that the second person must give up their own—and this is, in effect, what the emotional blackmailer intends. To the emotional blackmailer, the second person does not exist as a person in their own right. They only exist to gratify the blackmailer's demands.

In any relationship with an emotional blackmailer, the people being blackmailed are not expected to have feelings of their own. Instead, they are expected to have and care about the feelings of the blackmailer. As you might expect, this does not leave much of a life for anyone else.

Guilt is a potent weapon, and emotional blackmailers wield it with astonishing ease. If it takes making you feel bad to make themselves feel better, then that is what they will do. The next time someone tries to make you feel guilty for refusing to do what they want, remember that emotional blackmail is not loving behavior. If they really loved and respected you, they would not ask you to do more than you are able or willing to do.

When dealing with emotional blackmailers, it is very important to create firm boundaries and to understand that you are not responsible for their happiness or their lives. Even if they threaten to kill themselves, it is *not* your responsibility. You can be kind and loving and say things like, "I love you, but it is not within my power to make you happy. Only you can do that. I can refer you to a counselor or agency that can give you the help you need—because I can't."

The most important thing you can do for yourself is to separate emotionally from an emotional blackmailer so that you can listen to your own feelings and needs. When you are a hostage to an emotional blackmailer, you are responding to *their* feelings and needs as if they were your own—but they are not.

Dismissal

A respectful person is considerate of the feelings, needs, and beliefs of others, particularly those they love. A person who readily dismisses your feelings, needs, or beliefs is being disrespectful, and if they do it all the time, then they are being toxic.

Your feelings, needs, and beliefs matter, but toxic people do not see it that way. In their world, *their* feelings, needs, and beliefs are the only ones that matter. In order to have a healthy relationship, however, you must be considered.

If it seems that you are always shelving your needs and preferences, then you are enabling a toxic attitude, which says, "You don't matter." If someone tries to dismiss your feelings as unimportant or—more likely—uncomfortable, then it is perfectly okay to own it. "I hear what you are saying, but I feel this way, and my feelings matter to me." You do not need to defend yourself, but you should not hide yourself, either. Denying your feelings is doing violence to yourself.

Denial

It is important to understand that all toxic behavior stems from an inner child who believes that they found a way to shield themselves from harm. Denial is a strong shield, and many people will pick it up to defend themselves from a painful truth. And if the truth is painful enough, the person who chooses denial may very easily believe their own fiction, no matter how much evidence exists to the contrary.

Denial may take many forms, but it always involves a failure to take responsibility for one's own actions. Often, abusive parents deny that any abuse occurred, which puts the burden on the abused to prove the truth. Even when the abuse is widely known, the abuser may continue to deny that they did anything wrong, and they may actually have convinced themselves that this is so. Emotional abusers, in particular, do not want to see the damage that may have resulted from their actions, and they may deny any wrongdoing until their dying day.

Sometimes people will cast about for a scapegoat. For example, instead of looking to themselves, they may look to heredity, environment, schooling, physical or mental illness, religion (or the lack thereof), or any other related factor to explain why someone in the family feels hurt. They do this because it is easier and less painful than looking in the mirror.

When dealing with denial, it is important to understand that it is not really your job to convince anyone of your truth. While a genuine apology would be lovely, it does not have the power to heal your hurt. Only you can do that. Have your truth, but do not make your healing contingent on whether other people accept it, because you have no control over that.

Conditional love

All that is toxic in the world stems from conditional love, which humanity has struggled with since we first picked up tools. Conditional love says, "I will love you if..." There is always a condition that must be met in order for the love to be returned. Now, there are many parents out there who will always love their children and cannot imagine placing a condition on that, and yet their actions will still occasionally add that little "if." It is something to be aware of in yourself, and in others.

If you go back through the list of toxic behaviors, there are many "ifs" in the love that is offered. "I will love you if you do what I want you to do. I will love you if you think the way I do. I will love you if stop being that way. I will love you if you stop having those feelings."

It is not loving to be disrespectful.

It is not loving to call you names.

It is not loving to want you to bury your feelings and needs.

It is not loving to expect slavish devotion at the expense of your own life.

It is not loving to make you feel guilty for being who you are.

It is not loving to deny the truth of your own feelings, whether they make sense to anyone else or not.

It is not loving to be unkind.

It is not loving to threaten you.

It is not loving to hurt you.

It is not loving to ask you to change yourself in order to make someone else comfortable.

The opposite of conditional love is *unconditional love*. This is the love of God, the Great I AM, the All There Is—however you conceive of it. This love has no conditions on it whatsoever. To love someone unconditionally means that there is nothing that they can ever do, say, think, or feel that would make you *not* love them. Think about that. It means total forgiveness. It means completely allowing that person to be who they are and how they are, without trying to change them in any way. It means accepting them completely, right now.

The enlightened masters, living and dead, were able to live from a place of unconditional love, so it is possible. It is not out of reach. Nevertheless, most of humanity still struggles with the conditions, so be kind to yourself as you walk this path. Your life is not a test. Your life is about finding your joy, in your own way and in your own time.

Toxic and abusive behaviors in the media

All of these toxic behaviors and more are not only on display in your personal interactions, they are projected in the media as well. This reinforces the idea that toxic and abusive behaviors are normal, which can make it even harder to recognize your inner child's suffering.

How many romantic novels or movies depict toxic relationships? Quite a few, unfortunately. Emily Brontë's own misanthropic anti-hero, Heathcliff, is often portrayed as a desirable romantic partner because of his passion for Catherine. In reality, the character is quite toxic and controlling, and his behavior in the second half of the novel (which is seldom portrayed on film), is brutal and abusive in the extreme. Heathcliff is no hero, and he is definitely no paragon of romantic passion. And yet, characters like him still appear in the media today, and the very toxic aspects of their professed "love" for the heroine are often whitewashed.

Other unhealthy behaviors are often glorified in print and film, as well, including out-of-control anger and base meanness. Very often, lazy storytellers take an "ends justify the means" approach, where anything goes as long as the hero gets what they want in the end. In reality, however, nothing good ever comes from such an approach.

Poor behavior is not relegated to fiction alone, however. Real-life toxic behavior plays out in the media every day, whether by politicians, athletes, movie stars, pundits, or people in your community. The newspapers and blogosphere are full of examples of people engaging in all kinds of abusive and toxic behavior. Can you imagine what it would be like if people everywhere began to heal their inner child? Can you imagine how much kinder the world would be? Can you imagine people everywhere living and operating from a place of joy? This is why this work is so important.

When using media of any kind, be critical. Use it as a learning experience. Learn to identify toxic and abusive behavior in others so that you can learn to avoid it in yourself and in your relationships.

Inner child abuse

Everybody is a genius. But if you judge a fish by its ability to climb a tree, it will live its whole life believing that it is stupid.
—Albert Einstein

Nobody abuses us more than we abuse ourselves.
—Don Miguel Ruiz

Would you tell a child that they are worthless, or stupid, or fat, or ugly? Would you punish them repeatedly or severely if they made a mistake? Would you deprive them of comfort or rest? Hopefully, you would not do any of these things to a child. So why do you do them to yourself?

Your inner child learned and helped to create a story about him or herself, and he or she tells it to you every day. That story may have come from toxic parents who dumped their anger and frustration on you, or it may have come from more subtle sources, such as playground taunts or TV ads. No matter what its origin is, however, your inner child is more likely to retell the negative parts of that story than the positive ones. The result of this continuing mantra is inner child abuse.

Everyone has an inner child who is abused in some way. No one is harder on you than you are. You may berate yourself, feel like a failure, feel unloveable, and feel hopelessly, fundamentally flawed. As a result, your inner child feels unhappy, unsafe, and unloved—and so do you.

Your inner monster

Abusing your inner child is not a comfortable idea. After all, he or she is a helpless child. To make the abuse you heap on yourself a little more palatable, you may subconsciously believe that you have an inner monster. And it is much easier to feel okay about abusing a monster rather than a child.

Your inner monster is your inner child's twin, the part of you that holds the anger, the resentments, the sadness, the grief, and the disgust. You probably don't like these feelings, so you don't like the inner person who has them, either. These feelings trigger reactions that you like even less. You may explode in anger, you may suffer in silence because you are afraid to speak your truth, you may have a hard time saying "No" and end up doing things you don't want to do, or you may repeat the patterns you hated with your own children. And when you do these things, you hate your inner monster a little more and punish yourself harshly for each transgression.

Who is this inner monster? Is it the "bad" part of you? Or do you make it "bad" with your judgments?

Your feelings are your feelings, and you have a right to them, even if they are negative. Negative emotions, like positive ones, are messengers. They are telling you something. Negative emotions are telling you what you need to heal. Since your emotions filter through your inner child, they must be understood from that perspective. Your grown-up, logical mind can understand things in a much more sophisticated way, but your inner child, whether they are two or ten, is less sophisticated. To understand your inner child, you must think like a child.

In truth, of course, your inner monster and your inner child are the same being. You may prefer to split off the "bad" part of yourself and shove it in the closet, but that is denial of what is. Those feelings are yours, and the sooner you own them, the sooner you can heal them.

To own your inner monster, you must bring it out of the closet, get to know it, and acknowledge its feelings. This is not something you will complete in a day. Exploring and releasing these feelings will take time and commitment.

Your inner angel

Underneath all the abuse you heap on yourself lies the person you really are: your inner angel. Your inner child—*you*—are an angel and a divine Spirit. It does not matter if your angel is joyful or angry or peaceful or depressed. Feelings are not wrong or "bad." You have an inner angel who feels. And this angel—your Spirit—is eternal, powerful, divine, and loved beyond measure. Healing your inner child also means discovering your inner angel.

You were born to believe that you are less than you are, that you are imperfect and separate from everything else. You believe this because you chose to have the experience of believing it. In part, it is a game—what better challenge for an infinitely powerful being than to pretend that they are not infinitely powerful?

In part, this is also a learning process, a method of spiritual growth. Some spiritual guides call this process "mastering limitation," and that is what you are doing: you are mastering the art of being what you are *not*—limited, powerless, unworthy, or unimportant. In order to do this, you have to believe it. And, miraculously, you do; we all do. You could say that people abuse their inner child because they are so successful at being human.

Part of the fun of this game of life, however, is waking up and remembering who you are. This happens for everyone in a different way, and at a different time. Waking up is a process that can last over several lifetimes, or it can happen in one. The time involved is not a reflection on the worth or evolvement of the soul; it is just part of the soul's perfect game plan.

To wake up is to heal, and this is where the rubber hits the road. In order to remember and understand your own infinite power and divinity, you must address your inner child's beliefs and feelings. If your inner child secretly believes that you suck, then all of the spiritual books and workshops in the world will not help you to believe differently.

Boundaries and boxes

I lost boundaries as a child that I didn't even realize it, and it wasn't talked about back then. You know, it was something you just buried and dealt with, and moved forward. What could you do about it?
—Marie Osmond

Boundaries allow you to get along in society and feel safe and respected. They define your personal, emotional, and spiritual space, and when someone crosses one of your boundaries, you are not going to be happy about it. Likewise, if you unknowingly cross someone else's boundary, they won't be enjoying your company, either.

Boundaries are a tricky thing, though. If you did not have a good role model, you may not be sure what they are or when you have crossed them. Likewise, you may not know how you should react when someone crosses yours. For example, if you had a parent who frequently invaded your boundaries, you may feel like you have no other choice than to allow these incursions into your space.

Boundaries become trickier still when you confuse them with boxes. While some parents may not provide any boundaries for their children, some provide too many. Having no boundaries is unhealthy, but being boxed in is no better. Every person has a unique, sacred purpose, and no one can fully express who they are from a box.

Boundaries

What is a boundary? Boundaries vary not only with the individual, but with the society or culture as well. Something that is acceptable in some societies is definitely not okay in others, and vice versa. In general, though, you can learn about societal and cultural differences before you travel, which will hopefully prevent a *faux pas*.

With individuals, however, you may have to sharpen your boundary senses and feel your way, at least to a certain extent. For example, some people do not mind physical touching or hugs. Then again, some do. If you have ever been hugged by someone you did not want a hug from, you know how uncomfortable this can be, for both parties.

In general, however, most people would agree that the following are examples of crossed boundaries:

- Unwanted physical contact of any kind (this boundary depends on the person; what's okay from your best friend is probably *not* okay from your boss)

- Handling or disposing of other people's possessions without asking

- Snooping through other people's things or private papers

- Not respecting other people's feelings or wishes, particularly when they say, "No"

- Imposing your beliefs on another person

- Discussing private or very personal information (yours or someone else's) in a public or professional setting

- Talking about things that make other people uncomfortable after they have let you know they do not want to hear it

- Betraying a confidence without a good reason for doing so

- Making references to a person's appearance, or something that the person cannot change, in a judgmental way

- Imposing on another person's space by overstaying your welcome or by leaving your stuff in their space

- Being chronically late for meetings, engagements, etc.

People with healthy boundaries are respectful of others. If the people in your life had healthy boundaries, then your inner child learned them. If the people in your life did not have healthy boundaries, then you not only did not learn them yourself, you suffered having your own boundaries encroached upon or ignored.

You can heal your boundary issues, but in order to do so, you must learn to defend your own as well as respect the boundaries of others.

Understanding and respecting the boundaries of others

If you did not learn good boundaries, then how do you know? In truth, it is hard to know without talking to people. You can begin by asking people you trust to give you loving, honest feedback.

If someone gives you upsetting feedback, your first impulse will probably be to discount it because it is painful to hear. The truth does hurt sometimes, but it is also a huge gift. Try to see it as such. Ask yourself: Is this true? Could my behavior be considered disrespectful? Give yourself time to integrate this feedback. It could take some time, but that is okay. This is not a race.

Of course, just because someone says something does not mean that it is the absolute truth—there is no such thing. Use your own powers of discernment. After all, some people may have a better sense of boundaries than you do, but some may not. Also, some people may have an axe to grind, so their feedback may not be as helpful as you had hoped. But you cannot know if the feedback is helpful or not if you are evaluating it from a purely emotional place. If you are upset with what you heard, you are not in a clear place to discern anything.

You can also get feedback on your behavior simply by being more observant. When people become upset, whether they say so or not, what happened? Was it something that you said or did? Maybe it had nothing to do with you. But how can you be sure?

If you find yourself in an uncomfortable situation, and you are not sure why, just ask some questions. For example, you can say, "I'm sorry. Did I do or say something to upset you?" No matter how they respond, remember that they are giving you a gift, and you will be best able to hear it if you can remain calm and open.

Dealing with people who have no boundaries

Everyone has to deal with people who have no boundaries. At best, such people may add stress to our lives. At worst, they may create a hostile environment. So what do you do?

In general, you are most likely to have a problem when you don't really understand what your own boundaries are, so you don't know when someone has crossed them. So the first step is to figure out your own boundaries.

That drives me crazy!

When we feel really bothered by a particular person or behavior, it may indicate a boundary issue for us. What is it, exactly, that drives you crazy? Do you know? You may not at first, but writing about it in a journal might help you to find out.

For example, what if something upsets you, and you express how upset you are. If the other person says, "Oh, you're making a mountain out of a molehill. You shouldn't be upset," then you might feel even *more* upset than before. Why? Because the other person negated your feelings by telling you that you should not be upset at all. This is disrespectful because it feels like they are saying, "Your feelings don't matter."

I feel upset!

Your feelings are always your barometer for what is really going on. If you are upset, then look at that. It is very common for a crossed boundary to be an emotional trigger for your inner child. Anything that feels disrespectful or dismissive is likely to trigger an old wound. Respect your feelings when they arise. They will tell you what the problem is.

Sometimes a crossed boundary is actually an attempt by another to take control of a situation—and take control of you. For example, if someone is chronically late, then they are in complete control of the situation, while you wait for 15 minutes or more, fuming. The underlying message is, "I'm in control, and I don't respect your time."

Likewise, if a person imposes their stuff or their presence on you while brushing aside your protests, then they are not only trying to control you, they are trying to bully you.

Now I'm angry at myself!

If you were brought up to believe that you had to be polite and courteous at all times, your inner child may believe that you cannot stand up for yourself and still be considered a good person. If so, you may feel that you cannot say, "No," to someone, even if they cross your boundaries.

As a result, you may feel angry—at yourself. You may convince yourself that you are angry at the person who imposed on you, but the truth is, you are really angry because you did not stand up for yourself and speak your truth. And so you unwittingly perpetuate the cycle of inner child abuse.

Boxes

*Some of the most wonderful people are the ones who don't
fit into boxes.*
—Tori Amos

*The reward for conformity was that everyone liked you
except yourself.*
—Rita Mae Brown

Healthy boundaries are necessary for your emotional,
mental, and spiritual well-being. Boxes, however, are just the
opposite. Boxes can be defined as boundaries at their worst: an
attempt to control and limit another human being. Of course, you
can never control another human being. You may earn some
influence, but you will never have control.

Voiced or unvoiced pressure to conform

Even very compassionate parents or guardians unwittingly
put their children in boxes. The people in your life probably had
spoken and unspoken expectations of you and encouraged you to
conform to *their* comfort zone. You were expected to feel a certain
way, behave a certain way, look a certain way, or think a certain
way. Some of these expectations may have been healthy attempts
to teach you boundaries. And some of these expectations may have
been unconscious attempts to mold you into someone you are not.

Sometimes the pressure to conform can be so strong that
you do not feel safe to be who you really are. As a child, you knew
intuitively what your parents would or would not approve of. If
you knew that they would disapprove of something that is a core
part of who you are, then you probably started hiding it even as a
child, because this was the only way that you could feel
emotionally safe. And you may have forgotten that you did this,
with the result that you hid your truth from yourself.

When children are encouraged to be someone other than who they are, a fearful, sad, grieving, or angry inner child is often the result.

The need to control is a safety issue

Everyone tries to control their world to some degree. We do whatever we think will make us feel secure, happy, and safe—emotionally safe, in particular. Driven by the allure of safety and order, we believe that we can control our environment, our jobs, the people around us, and even society or the world at large. This belief, however, is an illusion that only serves to mask inner pain, constant worry, low self-esteem, and a deep-seated unhappiness in ourselves.

Control is an illusion, because of course you have control over practically nothing. It is worth repeating: *you are not in control*. The only things you can control are the choices that you make and how you react to situations. That's it.

You are not in control of the other drivers on the road. You are not in control of whether your boss likes you. You are not in control of who your children are; you can't even control whether they take a nap or not. You can provide guidelines and discipline, but your kids will be who they are and make their own choices, ultimately. And you cannot "prevent" so-called bad experiences from happening to you because, in the divine order of things, you need these experiences to learn and grow. However, you *do* have control over how you react to these experiences and deal with them.

For example, you can decide to be so irked with that guy who cut you off on the turnpike that it ruins your day. Which only hurts...you. Or you can shrug it off and let it go. You can decide that a medical challenge means that your life is over. Or you can find the gift in the experience and choose to live each moment to its fullest, regardless of the outcome. You can choose to worry and be upset, or you can choose to be positive and make the most of what has been given to you.

If you felt "boxed in" as a child or misunderstood, incompetent, or fearful, it is likely that your parents were trying to control you in unhealthy ways. If you grew up feeling that you could not be trusted to do anything right, know that this feeling comes from your parent's own feelings of ineptitude. We pass on the feelings about ourselves that we do not heal.

Trust is the antidote

Why do we have the need to control things? The issue is largely one of *trust*—the lack of it. A control freak does not trust anyone. Some people are so distrustful of even their spouse and children that they feel like they have to do everything themselves—because no one else in the family "does it right." The result? A person who has overburdened themselves to the breaking point and cannot accept help—because they do not trust that anyone else will perform the tasks to their satisfaction.

So whom should you trust? Yourself, for one. And your own sense of internal knowing and power. Of course, your power has nothing to do with how many people agree with you or jump to attention when you enter the room. Your power is independent of other people and situations. Your power comes from the one within you, from your Spirit.

If you are trying to control your world, then you do not trust your own inner guidance. It will never steer you wrong, although your ego, the voice of your mind, will. Your ego is the one that replays old tapes, reminding you of how worthless and powerless you are, and how you could never succeed if you followed your heart. Your heart's voice is small and very quiet, and it is easily overridden by your head. It takes time and practice to hear what your heart says, and it also takes time to learn to trust it and ignore what your fearful ego has to say about it. For one thing, your inner child probably does not feel safe enough to trust yet, and he or she spent many years learning how *not* to trust. You can learn to trust yourself—and others—again, but first you must learn to feel safe.

9

Discovering and respecting your true feelings

I pay no attention whatever to anybody's praise or blame. I simply follow my own feelings.
—Wolfgang Amadeus Mozart

Just as your car runs more smoothly and requires less energy to go faster and farther when the wheels are in perfect alignment, you perform better when your thoughts, feelings, emotions, goals, and values are in balance.
—Brian Tracy

When you react without thinking, a feeling has taken control. This feeling is as old as your inner child, and it can suddenly induce a reaction in you because that is the path that this feeling always takes. A well traveled path becomes a road, and the ruts give testimony to the miles you have walked upon it.

When a path becomes a road in your body, your nervous system learns to react in specific ways to specific inputs. If certain words or actions act like a trigger to make you feel bad about yourself, then your response to this input may be to feel depressed, and the more you walk the road of depression, the more ingrained and rutted it becomes in your nervous system and in your body. Whatever wounds your inner child has, they have left their mark on your physiology. Changing them now means you must change your physical responses as well as your mental and emotional ones.

Your emotional houses

Feelings are like a color chart that God has given us.
—Keith Miller

Everyone has an emotional house that is full of rooms, and each room represents a different human emotion. Some people learn that it's okay to venture into most of these rooms. A given room may not be fun—take grief, for example—but they know they will survive it, and the world is still a safe place afterward. But many people grow up feeling that at least some of these rooms are not safe, and they should be avoided whenever possible.

Some people never venture beyond one or two rooms, however. For example, some people go into the Anger Room first, and then they find it hard to leave it.

It can be very difficult to allow yourself to feel grief, sadness, or even joy. A part of you may feel that if you open some of those other doors, your world will fall apart. And it is true: strong emotion can be overwhelming. This is why your inner child may have decided not to let you feel some of it.

The thing is, if you do not let yourself feel some of these scary emotions, then you end up not feeling *any* of them, including the happy ones.

Meditation: Explore your emotional house

Sit in a comfortable chair and relax. Take several deep breaths, inhaling through the nose, and exhaling forcefully through the mouth.

See yourself standing in front of a house. It is a familiar house that you have visited many times. The door is already open, inviting you inside.

As you walk inside the door, you feel comfortable in this room because it is always the first room you see.

What objects do you see? This room represents an emotion. How do you feel right now?

Walk through the house and explore all of the rooms and pay special attention to how you feel in each:

- What objects do you see?

- How do you feel in each room? What is the primary emotion that the room represents?

- Are you comfortable in the room, or do you feel anxious or upset?

- What thoughts or memories come up in the room?

As you explore your house, include all of the rooms, including the kitchen, bathrooms, or even storage rooms.

If at any time a room is too overwhelming or upsetting for you, leave it and try again another time.

Your true feelings are your inner child's feelings

Children develop feelings and behaviors that seem irrational on the surface. They do not think about why they respond the way they do—they just respond. They cannot tell you why they feel the way they do or why they act out. So it is up to you, as an adult, to understand where your inner child's reactions are coming from. If you feel that nothing you do is ever good enough, then your inner child may have learned to believe this because you had a perfectionist parent who never recognized your good efforts or who was never satisfied by your efforts. A child cannot make this connection, but you, as the adult, can.

To help you with this process, keep a journal and try the following exercises:

- **Identify your feelings.**
  Write down whatever comes to mind, as many feelings as you can identify. Are you often frustrated? Do you

lose your temper (anger)? Do you feel depressed? Do you sometimes feel like crying, but you don't know why? Are you happy, at least sometimes? What does it look like when you are happy?

- **Identify triggers for your feelings.**
  For each emotion that you listed, write down the circumstances in which they come up for you. When you feel frustrated, what happens? Do you feel unheard? Or when you feel angry, what triggers this for you? Feeling criticized, feeling put down, feeling disrespected or unheard?

- **Create a loving response for your inner child.**
  For each trigger that you identify, create a loving way to respond when these feelings come up for you. You can write affirmations, or you can simply tell your inner child that they are safe, that you are the parent now, and that you love them. If feeling criticized is a trigger for you, you might respond with, "I am not criticizing you, and my opinion is the only one that matters. You are perfect right now, and I applaud your perfect efforts."

- **Talk to your inner child every day.**
  Take some time each day to sit quietly with your inner child. Give him or her the positive reinforcement they need to heal. Remind them that they are safe now, and that you have their back. Then ask them how they feel in that moment. Let them know that you hear them and that it's okay to feel like that.

Once you have identified how your inner child really feels, you can begin to understand why they feel that way and why you react the way you do in given situations. With this understanding, you can begin the healing process.

Whenever you are hard on yourself or beat yourself up, stop. Stop and try to identify the feeling that is lying underneath the abuse. If possible, write about it in your journal. But above all, forgive yourself. Forgive yourself for beating yourself up. Forgive yourself for having an uncomfortable emotion and affirm that it is okay to feel negative emotions. Emotions are divine messengers. Thank the emotion for teaching you about yourself. See it as a gift.

Reparenting your inner child

*Most of us become parents long before we have stopped
being children.*
—Mignon McLaughlin

Reparenting is the process of integrating your inner child
with your grown-up self. Ideally, it involves replacing all of your
false gods with the only god that matters: you. You are your own
authority figure. Everything you say, think, want, or feel *matters*.

Reparenting does not mean that you no longer honor, love,
or appreciate your own parents. A healthy adult is one who has
separated enough from their parents to become a happy,
competent, and autonomous human being in their own right. This
means that you are comfortable taking the reins in your own life
and making your own decisions, even if they do not always work
out as you had hoped. If you have benevolent parents, you may
find that your relationship with them improves, and they become
more like friends. But if you have toxic parents, it means that you
learn to draw healthy boundaries and defend them, if necessary.

Being gentle with yourself

Healing your inner child is not something that is going to
happen overnight. You did not develop your feelings and learn
your patterns all in one day, so you will not resolve them all in
one day. Nevertheless, your inner critic is likely to berate you for

any perceived "failure" to heal (or "fix") yourself, which only makes the process longer and more painful.

When you find that you are being hard on yourself, please stop. Breathe deeply. Think. Gain some perspective. Anything that you perceive as a failure is another step on the healing path, and you will learn from it—*unless* you use it as a cudgel to beat yourself with. Remember, abusing yourself only reinforces the negative patterns you do not want any more. Be as gentle and as loving as possible. With practice, patience, and love, you *will* form new habits and patterns and heal your inner child.

Above all, remember to treat yourself as lovingly as you would any child. You are loved beyond measure, and you are worthy of being treated gently and compassionately. Give this gift to yourself. Do not worry if you forget or have bad moments or react thoughtlessly. We are all children, learning every day. There is no failure in what we do. It is all learning process.

Taking responsibility

As you begin to reparent your inner child, you become responsible for your own well being. Reparenting means that you are stepping up to the plate for your inner child. Your inner child may feel abandoned, neglected, betrayed, or a host of other things, but it is critically important that your inner child knows that they can trust you now. Remember: you are competent, grown up, and safe, and *you can do this*.

The single biggest roadblock to healing is believing that everything that is wrong with your life is someone else's fault. If the responsibility for your life is not yours, then you get to say things like, "If only my spouse would help around the house, my life would be less stressful," or "If only my boss would recognize what a great job I'm doing, I'd get the compensation I deserve." These "If only" statements place the blame for your problems on someone else, never on you. Worse still, these beliefs take away your power to do *anything* to resolve your problems, and they give your power to other people instead.

Blaming other people for your problems leaves you completely powerless, because the "cure" for your problems then rests with something you absolutely cannot control: other people's behavior. If you have spent a lot of your life waiting for other people to change, you are probably still waiting, and will be indefinitely.

The one thing you can control, however, is your choices and how you react to the things that happen to you. If something is not working in your life, own it. When you own it, you also own the power to change it. If your spouse's behavior is making you crazy, they are probably not going to change. But you can. You can choose to react differently, you can choose a different resolution, and you can choose to either accept your spouse as they are or move on if it's a real deal-breaker for you.

When you take responsibility, you open the door to other possibilities, including the possibility that the issue is not as big as you thought it was. In fact, the issue is probably a trigger for some of your inner child's pain. When you stop blaming others, you can get to the heart of your inner child, and real understanding can begin.

So, to begin healing, your first step is take responsibility for everything in your life, including your thoughts, feelings, and beliefs.

Changing negative patterns

When it comes to healing your inner child, one thing is certain: you cannot *think* your way out of it.

The emotional and reactive patterns that you learned as a child will not disappear with thought or willpower alone. They are a part of your nervous system. You *can* change them, but you must be patient with yourself.

Intellectual understanding is necessary to help you understand why you react and feel the way that you do, but it is not enough. You must integrate this understanding emotionally and physically as well, which takes time.

The following technique is designed to help you change your reactions over time. For best results, do it whenever you think about it. You may do this for weeks, months, or years. Remember: you are literally reprogramming your body's automatic responses. To be successful, you must make new choices and repeat them many times.

Step 1: Recognize the pattern that you want to change

The first step is to recognize and acknowledge the pattern that you want to change. What happens when your inner child takes control?

If you react in a way that you do not like or that seems all too familiar, stop what you are doing and check in. How do you feel right now? What triggered your reaction? Did you feel stressed? Criticized? Disrespected? Unheard?

Identify what happened and why you reacted the way you did, if you can. You may not know at first, and this is okay. Keep a journal to help you understand what your patterns are. Over time, you will find the answers.

Step 2: Learn to recognize when the pattern is occurring

The second step is to learn to recognize when the pattern is occurring so that you have the opportunity to change the dynamic.

Slow down. Your patterns are most likely to emerge when you are busy or stressed, because these are the times when you will react without thinking. You may have a lot of things on your plate, but you can still slow down. The stress you are feeling is due to demands that *you*—and you alone—have placed on yourself.

When you slow down, you can observe your feelings and your body. Your feelings are your barometer for what is really going on. Your body is mirroring the stress of your emotions, so it is probably tense, and your breathing is probably shallow.

Slow down to allow the stress of the moment to leave you. Take slow, deep breaths. Relax your body. If you can relax your physical body, it will automatically change your mental and emotional state.

Step 3: Connect with your grown-up self

The third step is to connect with your grown-up self. Remind yourself who is in charge. Reassure your inner child that you are now grown up, safe, loved, and competent. Tell your inner child that *you* are the parent now, and you will handle things from here on out.

Step 4: Connect with others

Once you have slowed down and taken control as the grown-up, connect with the people around you (or with your own Spirit if you are alone). If you were having an argument, or if you felt hurt, take responsibility for that. You can say, "Wow, I felt really angry or hurt or upset when you said that, and I know I could have reacted better. Let's start again."

Standing up for your inner child

It takes courage to grow up and become who you really are.
—e.e. cummings

When you were a child, if you were lucky, someone had your back. Ideally, your parents were there to back you up or stand up for you when you needed them. But even if you had that advantage, an important part of growing up is learning to stand up for yourself: to the playground bully, to your best friend, to the adult who misunderstood you, to your partner, or even to your parents.

Depending on your upbringing, however, you may not have learned this skill. If your parents had no boundaries, then they probably intruded on yours so often that it not only feels normal, but it also feels like you are not supposed to defend them. And if you had angry or defensive parents, standing up for yourself might have carried a lot of risk. In those circumstances, your inner child may have wisely decided that it was better to lie low and avoid being seen than to stand up for yourself.

As an adult, however, it is vitally important that you learn how to stand up for yourself. If you cannot do this, who will? When you stand up for yourself, you are communicating to your inner child that you are worthy of respect, and that you matter. When you begin to believe this, an amazing thing happens: other people come to believe it, too. Not everyone will, but the right people will.

Living as though you matter

Most people typically do not like people who always put their own needs before the needs of others, but in your desire to be "a good person," you may often go to the other extreme, in which everyone's needs come before your own. This is not only out of balance, it is a form of self-deprecation that says to the Universe, "I am not worthy." As with anything you think or believe, the Universe will respond by creating a reality that matches your thought.

You may have learned from an early age that if you give, you are a good person. You may have also learned that sacrificing for others makes you a good person. "It is better to give than to receive," as the saying goes. And there is no question that giving is a great and necessary thing. It is how we expand beyond ourselves and share our divinity. But if you give from the well too often without replenishing the water, the well will go dry. When this happens, you suffer and are left with nothing to give. Everybody loses.

> *The sacrifice which causes sorrow to the doer of the sacrifice is no sacrifice. Real sacrifice lightens the mind of the doer and gives him a sense of peace and joy.*
> —Mahatma Gandhi

Excessive giving and sacrifice can be a form of self-punishment stemming from a sense of worthlessness. If everybody in your life "always comes first," then you may believe, consciously or not, that you do not deserve to come first. This can happen to anyone, but it is very common with women who have families. Mothers are often the ones who "keep it all together" and put the needs of their family before their own, sometimes to the extent that they become depressed because their needs are not being met. Women in particular are socialized to believe that their primary function is to be a mother, and anything outside of that role is not as important. Of course, this can also happen with fathers, who may believe that their role as provider trumps their personal needs, too. These are just examples; everyone is susceptible to this kind of thinking.

Some people who give too much, without receiving, stay very busy. Often, this "busyness" is a way to avoid being still: if you are too busy to sit with yourself, you might not notice that you are not happy. You might not notice the things in your life that are not working. You might not notice the things that you really want or need to change. Sometimes, sacrifice helps you hide from yourself.

In order to heal and be happy, you must learn to receive. Paradoxically, this may be much harder than learning to give for you. The act of receiving gracefully and gratefully is one of the most important spiritual lessons that you can learn. When you receive, you affirm to the Universe, "Yes, I deserve this. Thank you." When you receive, you are filling your personal well. As it begins to overflow, you can share that overflow with the people around you, which then returns to you again, refilling your well, only to be given yet again. This is the divine cycle of giving and receiving. This is the divine cycle of our abundance.

Abundance also encompasses time, energy, and nurturing. When you matter, you give yourself all of these things. You give yourself the time to be, or to do whatever fulfills you. You take care of yourself, whether by doing yoga, meditating, or going dancing. You allow yourself to have the things that energize you and that make you feel nurtured. You allow others to do these things for you as well. Maybe you let someone else make dinner or do the laundry, even if that means it doesn't get done "perfectly." What *is* perfect is knowing how to receive with gratitude, so that you can give back in your own perfectly imperfect way.

Learning to say, "No"

How many times have you said "Yes" when your heart was screaming "No?" Probably quite a few. There are many reasons why you might do the opposite of what you really want to do, including the following:

- You believe it is impolite to say "No."

- You're afraid that if you say "No," people will think less of you or think that you are selfish.

- You genuinely want to help or please your friends or family, and you feel obligated to say "Yes" every time they ask anything of you.

- You were never given the option of saying "No."

- You try to say "No," but feel bullied into saying "Yes" because you do not have a good enough reason not to do what is asked of you.

- Saying "Yes" means avoiding a conflict.

The problem with saying "Yes" when you mean "No" is that you end up regularly doing things that you do not want to do, which makes you feel resentful and unhappy. Worse, it may even mean that you end up doing things that your heart or your conscience finds objectionable. Saying "Yes" may also mean that you end up doing something that takes you away from your true purpose in this life—and only you can know and understand what that is and how that feels.

Saying "No" is compassionate

No matter what your reasons are for avoiding "No," you must learn to speak it when you feel it. This does not mean, however, that you must be rude or overly frank when you do it. If someone asks you to do something, it is perfectly acceptable to say, "I'm sorry, I can't help you with that. Have you tried asking Debbie? She really enjoys doing that." Of course, context matters, so if it is just a matter of timing, you can say, "It's just not a good time right now, but hit me up again later, okay?"

Saying "No" is an act of compassion for *you*, because doing so honors your true feelings. It is your way of affirming to yourself, "I matter."

Saying "No" is also an act of compassion for the people in your life. If you do something grudgingly, you are not giving your best effort. Your resentment will color everything, and that is no gift. You can say "No" lovingly and firmly. Give that gift.

"No" does not need a defense

Sometimes you may try to say "No" only to find that the other person wants to know why you will not help them. As you fumble for a clear rationale (feelings are very difficult to explain logically), the other person may become very aggressive and tear down your arguments in an attempt to make you do what they want you to do. If you had parents who excelled at this, you may give in pretty quickly or not even bother trying to defend yourself. So you say, "Yes," and add another resentment onto the pile.

The way around this is to realize that you never have to defend your decision. "Because I don't want to" is the only explanation you need to provide. It is always sufficient.

If you know that the person you are dealing with wants to break you down until you say "Yes," then simply do not give them that opportunity. Just say, "No," and walk away. Your answer does not have to satisfy *them*, only *you*.

Saying "Yes" as a compromise

There may be times when you need to say "Yes" when you do not want to. Compromise is essential in all relationships, after all. But if you do, make sure that there is some give on the other end. Make a deal. For example, you can say, "You know, I'm really swamped right now, but I can see that you're in a tight spot. I'll give you a hand with this, and then later you can help me with my project."

The important thing to remember is that you should not be a doormat, but you also should not be overbearing in your defense of your boundaries. Reciprocation is important, and that means you must learn to take as well as give.

Exercise: Becoming comfortable with "No"

If you struggle with the word "No," then it is time to make it your friend. Every day, spend some time alone in front of a mirror and say, "No." Say it with different voices, different inflections, and different tones. Whisper it. Use a normal tone. Scream, "NO!" Say it in every way you can think of.

You may feel ridiculous at first, but this exercise will help you to find your own voice. Speak for yourself! Giggle, laugh, shout. Have fun with it.

Continue this exercise until you feel comfortable enough to start speaking it for yourself.

Speaking your truth

Trust your own instinct. Your mistakes might as well be your own, instead of someone else's.
—Billy Wilder

Most people think that speaking their truth is about stating their opinions. It isn't. Speaking your truth goes much, much deeper than that. In the grand scheme of things, opinions are irrelevant, but your truth is everything.

What is your truth? You probably think you know, but chances are, you are missing pieces of it. Your truth is about who you really are and who you came to be, without regard to culture or social conventions. That's the part that gets scary, and that's the part that makes you hide your truth from yourself.

No other person can truly oppress you, but you can oppress yourself. If your inner truth says that you need to be an artist, but you become a lawyer because you feel obligated to, then you are suppressing your truth. In this case, speaking your truth means saying, "My heart tells me that I am an artist, and I won't be happy doing anything else." Speaking your truth means supporting your words with actions, so using this example, you would do whatever it takes to pursue your dream of becoming an artist. And finally, speaking your truth means having the courage to stand in your truth and trusting that the Universe will support you in it, because this is who you came here to be.

Of course, this is a simple example, and your truth is about more than your professional calling. It is about the choices you make every day. Your truth may say that you need to leave a relationship. Sometimes it says that you want a relationship with someone else. Or maybe it means you really do want children after all, even though your partner does not. Or maybe it tells you that you need to move.

To live in your truth is to be in integrity with yourself. If you do not do this, you betray yourself, and that is the worst kind of betrayal. But you cannot do this unless you really know what your truth is. To find out, you have to be completely honest with yourself, and this requires courage. It means hearing the answers you do not want to hear. Spirit always answers your prayers and questions; you just may not like the answers that come, so you ask again, hoping for a different answer.

Meditation: Discovering your truth

Sit in a comfortable chair and relax. Take several deep breaths, inhaling through the nose, and exhaling forcefully through the mouth.

As you breathe, a column of golden light descends through the top of your head and into your heart, where it coalesces in a ball of light. With each breath, this golden ball increases in size.

You gradually become aware that this golden ball and the golden column of light stretch upward toward infinity, connecting you with your own divine Spirit. Your Spirit communicates directly with your heart.

Gently ask your mind to withhold judgment and to step aside so that you can hear the answers to your questions. Be open to any answers that may come.

When you are ready, ask your Spirit a question to help you clarify your feelings about a particular subject. Then wait for the answer.

You may find that you already knew the answer. That is okay. You may be surprised or even disappointed by the answer. Try not to judge the answer—right now, you just want to receive the information clearly.

When you are ready, ask another question, or gently return to the world.

Demystifying your gods

God is not present in idols. Your feelings are your god. The soul is your temple.
—Chanakya

As you learn to stand up for your inner child, you will find yourself standing face to face with your gods, whatever or whoever they are. Because you gave them a god-like authority over you, it may feel uncomfortable, difficult, or even impossible to face them down and stand up for yourself now. But in order to heal and create joy in your life, it is essential that you stand up for your needs, even if it means defying your gods. Depending on who or what your gods are, however, that may sound pretty scary.

In order to stand up to your gods, it helps to demystify them. In L. Frank Baum's *The Wizard of Oz*, the wizard himself was a god-like being who seemed to be all-powerful and all-seeing, so Dorothy and her friends were greatly intimidated by this seeming omnipotence. But as we discovered only after the four travelers were sent on a wild and dangerous detour to the castle of the Wicked Witch of the West, the wizard was really just a little old man who held no more power than any of our heroes. Dorothy, the Scarecrow, the Tin Man, and the Lion put their lives in danger because they believed that the wizard was the only one who had the power to help them, and they were afraid that they would never get what they wanted if they did not do as he asked. Because they believed these things, the wizard could control them.

There is always a "man behind the curtain," and when you create a god, you also give it whatever power you think it has. If money is your god, then it holds your life hostage only because you think it can. If your parents, friends, or other loved ones are your gods, then they control you. Is this okay with you? If the answer is no, then it is time to pull back the curtain.

Transforming parents from gods into people

It is very common for parents to be gods, so if yours are, give yourself a break. You were doing what comes very naturally for kids: idolizing your parents. There is nothing inherently wrong with this, but it can cause problems if it continues into adulthood.

When you were a kid, you wanted your parents' approval. This is completely normal. Everyone wants the most important people in their life to not only love them, but to *like* them. When your parents approve of you, you feel that they like you, personally. That feels good.

However, when parents are gods, you may crave their approval in ways that are unhealthy. You may alter your personality or make choices and decisions based on what *they* would like you to do, instead of what *you* want to do. When this happens, you are no longer following your own heart and your own path; instead, you are following theirs. Consequently, you may feel angry, resentful, unhappy, or even depressed because you are not being true to yourself.

If you have benevolent parents, they are probably your gods simply because you love and respect them. In some ways, it is more difficult for the children of benevolent parents to stop deifying them than it is for the children of toxic parents. This is because children of benevolent parents feel that they would be disloyal to their parents if they believed that they were anything less than perfect. Logically, of course, this does not make sense. No one is perfect, and everyone has their issues and shortcomings. But some children fear that if they admit to their parents' failings, then it must mean they do not love their parents, or that they have betrayed them.

If you know you have toxic parents, however, you are probably aware of their shortcomings, but the fear of betraying even a toxic parent can keep them up on the pedestal. Some people, however, have toxic parents but have a hard time admitting this to themselves—again, it feels like a betrayal to think or say, "I have toxic parents." But admitting to the truth of your family dynamic does not mean that you have to stop loving anyone. It is the truth that will set you free and humanize your gods.

Of course, there is another possible reason why your parents may be your gods: because they want to be. Some parents subconsciously want to control their children's lives. They want to be adored. They want to have the last word. In short, they want *you* to validate them. Again, this is not a conscious plot. In cases like this, it is their own inner child talking. It is their own inner child's needs they are trying to fill through toxic means. At heart, such parents are deeply insecure in themselves and feel that if they can be everything in your universe, then they are smart and important, and they matter.

If your parents habitually control, bully, or manipulate you, then they want to be your gods, and they raised you to have this belief as well. It is therefore up to you to step back and see them as fallible human beings and develop new ways of relating to them. Why are they toxic? They probably endured toxic upbringings themselves. You can have compassion for that, but know this: *their misery is not your responsibility. Their happiness is not your responsibility.* They have every opportunity to heal from their past, as you have from yours.

Learning to relate to mere mortals

If you are like most people, you are tired of feeling like a six-year-old whenever you go home to visit your parents. How do you change that? The only person you have control of is you. To change your family dynamic, you must change yourself. This will take time, patience, and hard work on your part.

In order to be an adult, you must learn how to make your own decisions without caring about what your parents or other family members are going to say. If you decide that you want to quit your job and become an artist, then do it. If your parents complain, you will have to learn how to disengage before it becomes an argument. Just say, "I'm sorry you feel that way, but this is what I have to do." End of discussion. If they attempt to pull you in to another argument (and they may), you must remain firm in your decision to end the discussion. Toxic parents in particular are masters of trying to use "logic" to convince you why they are right, and you are wrong. *The only way you can deal with this is to stop engaging in the argument.* You don't have to prove *anything* to your parents.

Basically, to be an adult, you must take responsibility for yourself. You must be okay with not having their approval, because you may not get it. You may need to mourn the fact that you will never get this. What child does not want their parents' approval? But you are *not* a six-year-old anymore; you are a grown-up, so you *can* move through this.

As you are able to detach from your parents, to de-tangle yourself from the daily Family Drama, you will become the adult you want to be. But be aware that when you start this process, you will change the energy in your family. You are changing the family dynamic, and this will feel uncomfortable to everyone who is invested in it. Your family will work even harder to pull you back in to your old role, whether you were the peacemaker, the "good kid," or the family dumping ground. Some family members may even turn on you. Be prepared to stand your ground. If you give in, nothing will change, and you will severely impair or halt your healing process. Healing requires courage. No matter what happens, you are never alone, and the people who matter the most in the long run may not be from your family of origin.

As you stand up for yourself and disengage from the Family Drama, something remarkable will happen: you will begin to recover your long-lost self-esteem. You will be able to walk the road to your happiness.

Taking your power

The most significant step that you can take to heal your inner child is to take your own power. Paradoxically, this is something that is really scary for your inner child to do, so you will have to help him or her in the process.

When you were a child, you did not have much power. As you grew, however, you gained the power to make certain choices and decisions—possibly too many at some times in your life, or too few. When your choices did not work out the way you hoped or expected, you may have been taught to simply try again. Or you may have learned that if you "failed" in some way, all hell would break loose. In toxic households in particular, any perceived failure or imperfection can have scary consequences. Children from such households learn to fear their power because making a decision could turn out badly, so they learn to defer to others.

When you always defer to the wishes and opinions of others, however, you are not living for yourself. You are not empowered. Instead, someone else has the power to make the decisions in your life. This is never healthy, and if the people who are thus empowered have toxic behaviors as well, then you are probably pretty miserable. How do you get out of this trap?

Dethroning your gods

To take back your power, you must first dethrone your gods. Recognize that you gave them the power they have over you. Do not blame yourself or feel guilty for this, because whatever you did as a child, you did to protect yourself and survive. Have compassion for this.

When you decide to take back your power, it does not mean that you stop listening to or respecting the thoughts and opinions of others. You can be respectful, you can cooperate, and you can compromise where needed, but know that you as an individual hold the keys to your own happiness. Yes, you will need buy-in from others. You may need a plan. Change need not occur overnight. It seldom does, nor is it always desirable. But *own* your happiness. Own your feelings. Own your power. Know that your choices are yours, no matter how much pressure you may feel to act against your wishes.

If your gods are circumstances or things, you must take your power back from them as well. If you hate your job but feel like you can't quit, you are giving your power away. If you feel like your boss is the one who is making your life miserable, you are giving your power away. In these instances, you are abdicating all responsibility for your own choices and condition. There is *always* another choice you can make—you just may not like having to make it.

If you give your power to other things, you are enabling your own passivity. Life just "happens" to you. "It wasn't my fault; it's out of my hands," you might say. And then you become a victim. "I'm not happy, but I guess I never will be. I can't change jobs because of the mortgage. I can't be a musician because I have a family to support. I can't take a vacation because I don't have enough money. I can't take any time for myself because I have so much that I 'have to' do." In this way, you limit your world by limiting your power.

Ceremony: Releasing your gods

Write down the gods that you have identified and briefly describe the ways in which they have taken control in your life. Once you have identified your gods and the role they play in your life, you can release them and take back your power. Recognize that you gave them the power they have over you. Do not blame yourself or feel guilty for this, because whatever you did as a child, you did to protect yourself and survive. Have compassion for this.

Take the page that describes your gods and create a ritual that has meaning for you so that you can release them. For example, you might do any of these things:

- Light a candle.

- Acknowledge each god and thank them for the role they played and the lessons they brought to you.

- If the god is something you no longer need in your life, tell it that you release it with love.

- If the god is something you will still have in your life (such as money or food), tell it that you are taking control now, and that it is no longer more important than you are.

- Tell your inner child that you were not wrong to have these gods; they served a purpose, but you can release them as gods now.

- Tell your inner child that you are a competent and capable grown-up who does not need to give away your power.

- Write words of love, gratitude, and release on the paper.

- Ceremonially release your gods by blessing or clearing the paper, burying the paper, or burning it in a fireplace or in some other safe way.

Learning to love yourself

I wish I could show you, when you are lonely or in darkness, the astonishing light of your own being.
—Hafiz

Learning to love yourself is the Holy Grail of all healing. And yet, it also feels like the Mount Everest of all healing: gigantic and unattainable. It is absolutely possible to learn to love and accept yourself, but as with all things, it is a journey, not a destination.

Most people want to learn to love themselves, but they have no idea where to begin. How do you even begin to believe something that you do not believe today? You start by practicing. Music virtuosos are not born; they are made. You can become a virtuoso of self-love, but you must start with what you have today and build on that, consciously and patiently.

What conditional self-love looks like

As discussed previously in this book, conditional love is the grandmother of all toxic behaviors, and when you direct it at yourself, you are abusing yourself.

When conditional love is directed toward others, it says "I will love you if..." But when conditional love is directed toward yourself, it most often says, "I do not love you because..." That "because" ignores and negates every positive attribute in your being. Think about that. You undoubtedly posses thousands of countless gifts and beauties in your being, and you overlook every last one of them by choosing to focus on the handful of things you do not love about yourself.

The solution is to change this from a conditionally loving statement to an unconditionally loving statement. "I love you because…" is a good way to start, so that you can shift your focus from the things you do not love in yourself to the things that you do. As you continue, however, you cannot simply ignore those things you do not love about yourself. As long as you hate anything in yourself, you are loving yourself conditionally: "I love myself, except for these things." Remember, there are no exceptions in unconditional love.

The inner child, and by extension the ego, is a master at finding ways to disapprove of itself. You have done it for so long that it does not even occur to you that it is harmful. It just feels like who you are and what you do. Here are some examples of conditional self-love:

- I would be beautiful/handsome if…

- I'm a terrible person when I…

- I wish I were like him/her.

- I hate it when I do that!

- I can't seem to do anything right.

- I failed!

All of these criticisms are really judgments that you have made about yourself. Where did they come from? Your imagination? The answer is a bit more complex. The judgments that we form about ourselves or anyone else are rooted in our culture and environment. The beliefs and judgments of your family, community, and society are passed along to you, and you absorbed them like a sponge when you were a child. They lie there still, in your subconscious mind, forming your views.

Body judgments are the most common, and we are surrounded by media that purports to show us what is beautiful and healthy. Our families do the same thing, perhaps more subtly. The things that we value as a society are also thrust upon us in the most mundane interactions. Wealth, products, status, IQ, career, and specific ideas or belief systems have become false gods for many, and no one is immune from the effects of being immersed in a culture that glorifies them. The result is that people learn to judge one another against the standards of those gods, but most importantly, people learn to judge themselves by those standards. If you believe that you fall short (and your belief is the only thing that matters here), then you have created something to hate in yourself.

Social and cultural standards are arbitrary, and if you look at it from this perspective, judging yourself against any set of standards is judging yourself against something that is not real. Therefore, your judgment is not real, either—except that you give it value.

It is a painful thing to sit in judgment of yourself and carry it around with you. It literally makes you a prisoner of yourself. Because of this, you probably look outside of yourself for love and validation.

External validation as a replacement for self-love

When you cannot give yourself the love and acceptance that you and every other human being on earth needs, you look for it outside of yourself. This is called *external validation*, and you may look for it in your spouse, parents, children, friends, co-workers, the media, politics, church, you name it. Anything that appears to reflect you back to yourself in a favorable way is a good thing. But here's the rub: anything that reflects you back to yourself in an *unfavorable* way becomes a bad thing. The problem is that you cannot control whether someone or something will validate you or not.

For example, assume that you really love blue dragons. You paint them, you read about them, and you like to talk about them. There is nothing wrong with your preference or beliefs about blue dragons—it is just a part of you. If you meet someone new, and you mention that you really like blue dragons, they may respond favorably. They like blue dragons, too. This validates your experience and makes you feel good. It also makes you like this person better.

Now assume that you meet someone new, and they really hate blue dragons. This does not validate your love of them, so it feels bad to you, and you think, "If they don't like blue dragons, it means they don't like *me.*" To deal with this imagined rejection, your inner child may compromise and deny your true feelings: "Oh, blue dragons are okay, I guess, but they aren't my favorite thing." Another way in which your inner child may react is to decide that you just do not like this hater of blue dragons, and an opportunity to make a friend is lost.

This is just a lighthearted example, but if something means a lot to you and someone else criticizes what you love, you may take it personally. This is how the need for external validation rules your life: your need for it can override how you really feel and what you believe, causing you to make choices that you would never make otherwise. As a result, you compromise yourself.

When you take external validation into the realm of religion and politics, the inner child can get defensive very quickly. The inner child may see any kind of disagreement as invalidation of their beliefs, and this feels bad.

Although the inner child tries mightily, external validation does not provide a sense of love and acceptance. How can someone else give you what you cannot give yourself? Even if you get perfect external validation, and someone says, "I love you, you are perfect, you are good, you are beautiful, you are the best person I have ever known," your inner child tends to respond with, "I don't believe you." So the kind words feel good for a little while, but your inner child's judgment tapes keep rolling in your head until you cannot hear them anymore.

Naturally, your inner child most wants external validation from your parents and family. Who doesn't? You may spend your whole life trying to be the person that you think will "win" the approval of your family, only to discover at the end of it that you lived someone else's life in order to gain an approval that was never given. You may have to accept that you will never gain the unconditional love that everyone naturally yearns for from your family. It may simply never come. But remember, this is not a judgment on *you*. If anything, it is a judgment on them.

What unconditional self-love looks like

To be beautiful means to be yourself. You don't need to be accepted by others. You need to accept yourself.
—Thich Nhat Hanh

Unconditional love is based on acceptance of what is, right now. It does not place boundaries around itself. It does not exclude anything or make exceptions. It does not wait for a distant, more perfect tomorrow. It does not hate anything. It does not berate. It does not criticize. It does not even compare one thing with another.

Whatever it is you judge in yourself, whatever it is that you hate, you can choose to think about it differently. You can choose to stop judging it and to accept it. Even if you do not believe it at first, "fake it 'til you make it." Self-acceptance is a process.

Here are some examples of unconditional self-love:

- My body is perfect just as it is, right now.

- I am beautiful.

- My mistakes are valuable learning experiences.

- That didn't work out too well, but I'll do better next time.

- He/she said something really hurtful, but I know that what they said isn't true.

- I forgive myself.

- I appreciate myself.

Validate yourself

Your inner child sees everything that is wrong in you, but find the things that are right in you. They are legion. And instead of relying on external sources as your means of validation, validate yourself. Love yourself. Forgive yourself. Cherish yourself. Appreciate yourself. External critics do not matter. Your opinion of yourself matters.

Next, start to view all of those "wrong" or "bad" traits as gifts. For example, tell yourself, "My anger/toxic behavior is my gift because it has challenged me to grow and understand myself in new ways." You are not filled with "problems." You are faced with *challenges*. But avoid the trap of judging yourself for not having met those challenges well enough. By whose standard? One person's 100% is someone else's 10%, and it varies with the day and the circumstances. Give yourself a break.

Your beliefs about yourself define your world

Everything that you believe and feel about yourself gets projected outward. The world is reflecting your beliefs about yourself back to you. This is its purpose. If you fear being judged, this fear is projected outward, and as a result, you feel judged. If you have unresolved anger, then your anger is projected outward, and as a result, you feel wronged. If you believe you are wanting, then you experience that lack. If you believe you are unloveable, then you feel unloved. If you want to be kind to others, then be kind to yourself. It really does begin with you.

When you send a thought or a feeling to anything, it affects the thing itself. Thoughts and emotions are energy. Scientists are now starting to understand this on the level of quantum physics: the observer affects what he or she is observing. So when you continually think negative or hateful things about yourself, it affects you spiritually, mentally, emotionally, and even physically. A constant stream of unloving thoughts can literally make you ill.

Try to catch yourself and replace those unloving thoughts and feelings with something new and loving. When you think, "I hate my body," stop and send it love instead. Say, "I love you. I appreciate you. Thank you for serving me so well in this world. You are beautiful just as you are, right now."

If you find that you are berating yourself, stop. Instead, say something like, "I am really proud of the way I handle all of my challenges. I am learning every day. I am grateful for this opportunity to grow."

Remember, just because you have always believed something about yourself does not mean it is the truth about yourself. Most likely, your inner child absorbed those beliefs from external sources long ago. There is no reason for them to rule your life today. Find your true beauty and worth from within yourself. You are valuable, necessary, important, and loved.

Be authentic

The primary thing that keeps people from their joy and self-love is not being true to who they really are. In other words, they are *inauthentic*. Of course, like everything else about the inner child, being inauthentic is not a conscious decision.

As a child, you were inundated with external messages from everyone around you: parents, siblings, peers, teachers, and society at large. These messages told you in both subtle and unsubtle ways what you *should* believe, what you *should* think, and how you *should* behave. Deep inside yourself, however, you have always known who you were and who you came into this body to be. But this knowingness became entangled with the overlay of *shoulds* in your life, and you either became confused about who you were and what you wanted, or you may have forgotten it altogether in order to feel accepted and loved by those around you.

The single most important key to peace and happiness is to peel away those overlays and to identify who you are and how you want to be. This takes courage because the truth about yourself may be at odds with the way some people in your life see you or want you to be. Nevertheless, it is vital that you start this process and begin to live your life for you, and not for someone else. Nothing brings more sadness and disharmony to a soul than to attempt to be what it is not. So stop trying. Honor who you really are, and you will find fulfillment and joy. Most importantly, you will find it much easier to learn to love yourself, because you will be loving what you know in your heart to be true, instead of trying to love someone else's definition of who you should be.

As you discover your true self, you will find it unbearable or impossible to pretend to be anyone else. Being authentic will change your relationships, but the ones that truly matter will change for the better. If someone cannot deal with your authentic self, then it was not a very good relationship to start with. Remember, the most important relationship is the one that you have with yourself.

Meditation: Reconnecting with your true self

Self-love must come from within you, and sometimes that seems like an impossible goal. Stop believing that. It is very possible to achieve self-love, so create a new belief in yourself that allows for that possibility.

The following meditation is designed to give you the opportunity to connect more deeply with your own Spirit and who you are. It is also designed to help you clear your chakras and reconnect energetically. Do this as often as needed. Every meditation will be different, so you may want to record your experiences in a journal.

Meditation

Put yourself in a quiet state and breathe deeply, inhaling through the nose, and exhaling through the mouth.

As you breathe, focus your awareness on your physical body. Feel the life energy humming in every cell of your body. Listen to its song.

Feel your connection with the earth below you. Become aware of her Spirit, nourishing and loving you. You are here now in this home that is your body. Thank your body for its faithful service to you.

Now become aware of your energy body, which completely surrounds you. This energy flows with the rhythm of your breath.

Your emotional body flows around you to the right, clockwise. Feel it flow, and as you watch, see your heart chakra open and expand in your chest, growing until it is completely integrated with the flow of your emotional body.

How do you feel?

Ask your inner guide to show you what your natural state feels like, and then experience this feeling.

Now become aware of a flow of energy that moves around you to the left, counter-clockwise. This is your mental body. Notice the differences in this energy.

See your heart chakra connect with this mental energy as well. Now both energy bodies are moving synchronously with your heart.

What thoughts come to you?

Ask your inner guide what message you need to hear today, and then wait for the answer.

See a stream of light that pours into your energy bodies from above. It comes through your upper chakras, opening them one at a time, until it reaches your heart chakra, which opens even wider. From there, the energy continues downward, opening each chakra as it goes. The energy descends through your feet and into the earth. This energy is part of you, but it is not *of* you.

What thoughts or feelings come to you?

Who are you in this moment?

Sit in this energy as long as you like, and then come back when you are ready.

Making healthier choices

Be who you are and say what you feel, because those who mind don't matter, and those who matter don't mind.
—Dr. Seuss

Your past is your past, and what happened to you then is not something you can change. However, how you *think* about your past is completely in your control. You can choose to shift your thoughts. You can choose to forgive yourself and others, even if you no longer have a relationship with them. You can choose the things that make you happy. You can choose to *be happy*.

Forgiving

When you hold resentment toward another, you are bound to that person or condition by an emotional link that is stronger than steel. Forgiveness is the only way to dissolve that link and get free.
—Catherine Ponder

To forgive is to set a prisoner free and discover that the prisoner was you.
— Lewis B. Smedes

Forgiveness seems hard, because people tend to think it means that on some level you are condoning hurtful or toxic behavior. But that is not what forgiveness is about.

If you have not forgiven someone, you are carrying a grudge. Think about that phrase for a minute: *you are carrying a grudge*. Grudges are heavy things, and you are the one doing the carrying—not the person who wronged you. Grudges are also based on anger, and no matter how justified you may feel in having that anger, it is still *your* anger that is weighing you down. Your anger does not really hurt the other person in the long run— it hurts you.

Many people have said this, and it is true: forgiveness is a gift that you give to yourself. It does not mean that you have to tell the person you are forgiving or be friends with them again, or have any kind of relationship with them again, or even invite them over for coffee. The person you are forgiving does not even have to be alive; you can and should forgive those who have crossed over as well. Forgiveness simply means that you are putting down your anger because you are tired of carrying it.

Whatever anger you harbor for the actions of another, know that it is natural and normal. Recognize it; own it. But if you expect another person to fulfill a "requirement" before your anger can be healed, then you may wait a very long time. Why wait? Suspend your requirement. Recognize that the person may not be willing or capable of giving you the fulfillment you desire. Your healing comes from within *you*. It is available to you *now*. If you choose to hand your power to the other person and wait for them to dissolve your anger, then you will die angry. Many do. Ask yourself: is this what you want? Do you want to live in anger for the rest of your life? Your healing is in your own hands now. Take it. You can choose to forgive them, no matter what state of denial they may be living in. You can choose happiness and joy instead of anger. It really is all about you, not about anyone else.

Forgiving others is important, but it is even more important that you work on forgiving yourself. If that sounds difficult or impossible, remember that your core being is your inner child. Therefore, you are forgiving a child. You are forgiving a child who did the best they could and grew up with learned behaviors and coping mechanisms that were an attempt to remain safe. Let there be no judgment here.

If forgiving yourself and your inner child still sounds difficult, then begin by making the *decision* to forgive yourself, even if you do not yet feel convinced. Simply making this decision will allow miracles into your life.

Steps to forgiving yourself

To begin to forgive yourself, start with these four steps:

1. Forgive yourself for ever having believed such horrible things about yourself.

2. Forgive yourself for all of your perceived imperfections. They are not real; it is only your belief in them that gives them life.

3. Forgive yourself for beating yourself up. Recognize that you were abusing your inner child, and then forgive yourself for that, too.

4. Forgive yourself for believing that your past in any way defines who you are.

Of course, the very first rule is to decide, firmly, that you really are going to forgive yourself and that you are not going to judge yourself for not doing it "well enough." Having made this pact with yourself, you can start a dialogue with your inner child, which will help you to understand what needs to heal. It is incredibly important that you resist the impulse to use this new awareness as an excuse to beat yourself up further. This is counter-productive. You are on a voyage of self-discovery, and as the things that need to heal come into your awareness, use the experience as an opportunity to forgive yourself yet again. Self-condemnation makes things worse; self-forgiveness will set you free.

Writing a new story

If you are carrying strong feelings about something that happened in your past, they may hinder your ability to live in the present.
—Les Brown

How invested are you in your story? Does your life story define who you are? Who would you be without your pain? Do you know?

You cannot be happy if you continually think and speak of your pain. What happens when you recall a past grievance or hurt? In all likelihood, you get worked up and feel that hurt all over again. You relive the feelings of that moment. When you continually tell the story or bring it into your mind, you relive the painful past and bring it into your present moment. When this happens, your happiness goes right out the window.

If you are feeling stuck and you are continually living the pain of past events, then you need to tell a new story. If you are seeking validation for your pain (perpetual reassurance from others that you have a right to feel angry or upset), you may also be seeking excuses for remaining in pain. So, why would you want to remain in pain?

Your inner child grew up being accustomed to this pain, and no matter how unhealthy or uncomfortable it is, it is familiar. And the familiar feels safe, because it is known. It is very common for people who have been abused or lived in toxic households as children to attract the same kinds of relationships and situations as adults. They do this not because they enjoy it, but because they do not know what healthy, happy choices look like. Happiness is literally outside of their comfort zone. Is it outside of yours? When things start going well for you, do you sabotage them? When people try to get close to you, do you find reasons to make them go away?

Paradoxically, your story can also help to heal you, but in order for that to happen, you must not be invested in your story. Your story provides a way to connect with others. People are best helped by those who have had similar experiences and overcome them. The person who has healed a difficult past provides hope to others. They are a lighthouse, proof that healing is possible, even for those who have suffered greatly.

So, where are you in this process? Does your story keep you stuck?

Why are you telling your story?

The best way to determine where you are with your story is to ask yourself what your primary motivation is. Are you telling your story to gain sympathy? If so, it is probably holding you back. Write a new one! When you find yourself telling your old story, stop. Remember your new story and tell that one instead.

If you are telling your story to help others who have suffered similar pain, then your story is healing. We can all recognize a kindred spirit, and, no matter where they are in their healing process, your story lets them know that they are not alone. And any healing you have done, no matter how imperfect you think it is, will help that person and give them hope. When you do this, you will know how far you have come and how much you have healed, and you will know your gratitude.

Your story is important. Whatever you have experienced, you experienced for a reason. Everyone's path is different, but by sharing the fact that your healing exists at all, it helps others. And when you encounter someone who wants sympathy for their pain without doing anything to allow their joy to return, then you may become even more grateful for your own healing, and you heal some more.

Exercise: Creating a new story

Sit down with pen and paper and literally write a new story for yourself. Write, with as many details as you can imagine, what you would like the story of your life to be. Imagine the life that would give you the most profound joy. You may already be living some of that story. You may be yearning for some of that story. You may even think that such a story is not possible for you. Envision it anyway. Write it anyway. Then read it to yourself every day.

Each day when you read your new story, think of a small step that you can take that day to help make that story a reality, then do it. It does not have to be hard. It does not have to be complex. It could be as simple as taking a moment several times that day to say, "I love you" to your inner child.

Honoring your past

You can change your past by changing the way that you think about your past.

To heal your inner child, you do not need to forget your past—your old story. Instead, you are choosing not to live there anymore. Remember your past, but live now, and look ahead.

Your life is a boat you are sailing. Your past is the boat's wake. Do not focus on the wake, because if you do, you cannot see where you are going and cannot steer your boat. Face forward, and leave the wake behind you.

Understanding your changing relationships

Don't smother each other. No one can grow in the shade.
—Leo Buscaglia

As you release your past and any toxic influences, your relationships will be deeply affected. The more you heal, and the more joy you find for yourself, the more some people will fight you. People who are in a toxic relationship with you are comfortable with the toxic dynamic. When you stop interacting with them in this way, they are going to feel threatened. They are going to do everything in their power to pull you back into your old toxic loop. From their perspective, unconsciously, you are no longer "behaving" in the right way, or in a way that they can recognize. They will want the old, unhappy you back again because that is who they are comfortable with. This can be particularly difficult when these people are members of your family.

Fortunately, you will find that some people can grow with you. It may be difficult at times, but they will adapt. They will love you anyway. It may surprise you who these people are. Cherish them.

As you release the patterns that no longer serve you and as you find more and more joy, you will begin to attract new people into your life as well. Like attracts like, and new friends and loved ones will magically appear when you are ready for them. This is particularly reassuring when you have to let go of relationships with people who cannot accept the changes you are making in your life.

Releasing relationships that no longer serve you

At some point, everyone has to make the painful decision to let one or more relationships go. It may be a friend, possibly even someone you have known for many years. It may be a romantic partner. It may even be members of your family. There are as many reasons for severing relationships as there are people: feeling a profound sense of hurt or betrayal, simply drifting apart, discovering that you do not have much in common, or realizing that the thing that you placed such a high value on was toxic or demeaning to you in a way that you can no longer tolerate.

Whatever your reasons are for ending any relationship, it is important to know that you do not need to defend them. The person you are trying to release or mutual friends and family may go to great lengths to convince you that you are wrong, and that *you* are the problem. Also, you may find that when you start to defend yourself by giving reasons for ending a toxic relationship, those reasons are met with determined counter-arguments that are designed to make you give in by convincing you that your reasons are not such good reasons after all.

If you find that you must let someone go, do it with as few words as possible so that you do not get sucked into yet another toxic argument. You can be kind and loving, but above all, you must be firm and true to yourself. Have confidence that you are doing the right thing for you. Remember: the other person's happiness (or lack thereof) is not your responsibility. It is theirs. If they use emotional blackmail, see that for what it is. If they threaten you or themselves, take steps to make yourself safe, or contact a mutual friend on their behalf to help them out. But do not give in to any attempts to manipulate you. If you are ending a toxic relationship, it is a sign that you are on the path that will lead to your joy. Honor and respect that.

Releasing relationships with toxic parents

Can you have a relationship with a toxic parent? The real question here is probably, "Can you have a *good* relationship with a toxic parent?" And the answer, sadly, is probably not. If you have a toxic parent, they probably are not capable of having a good relationship. So you have to ask yourself, "What am I willing to put up with to have a relationship with my toxic parent?" Depending on the answer, you will know what to do.

You may be able to have a decent relationship with your parents if they are willing to go to counseling with you. If they will meet you even partway, there is hope. It will not work, however, if everything rests on your shoulders. That is not fair, and of course, it means nothing will change on their side. In that case, just know in yourself that your parents are the ones with the problem, not you.

Learn how to stand up for yourself using non-combative language. "I" language is typically best: "I feel hurt when you say things like that to me." This works a lot better than saying, "You are really hurtful." It puts the burden on you instead of on them, and they are more likely to hear what you are saying instead of simply shutting down. Start with, "I feel..." Depending on the parent, this may help to defuse some of the drama. If they are willing to go to counseling with you, it may even help your parents to find a new way to communicate with you.

On the other hand, all of the self-esteem, sense of personal responsibility, and "I" language in the world may not help you deal with some parents. Some toxic parents will simply adjust to the changes in you to find new ways of putting you down and making you crazy. Those who are physically abusive or suffer from personality disorders, in particular, are tough cases, and you will probably just have to accept that they are mentally ill, and nothing you can do will help you to have a normal, loving relationship with them. As a result, you may choose not to have a relationship with them at all. Cutting off your toxic parents can be an act of self-preservation, and in some cases, it is the only solution.

Dealing with people who do not understand

The lucky people who have loving, nurturing parents are unlikely to understand the pain that comes with having toxic parents. Your best friend in the world may look at you skeptically when you describe a "normal" interaction in your family. Likely, they will think you are exaggerating, and that you are simply at odds with your parents.

Worse still, if you find that you need to severely limit or cut off contact with your parents, your friends and family may look at you as if there is something wrong with you. "There must be something wrong with you to be so cruel to your poor mother/father," they may think. And this would be understandable—if we were talking about normal parents.

Toxic parents are generally very skilled at keeping the family secrets. They put on a good front as a normal, happy, upright family—perhaps even pillars in the community. Your toxic parent may charm the pants off of perfect strangers, your friends, and other relatives. All of which just appears to make you out to be the bad guy.

Again, though, you have no control over what the rest of the world does or thinks. You must look after yourself. No one else is going to do it for you. If you need to cut off your parents (or anyone else), then cut them off. Your real friends will not abandon you. The people who really care will support you. And other children of toxic parents will support you, too.

One of the best things you can do for yourself—to get validation for your feelings and to be able to heal—is to find a group of people who have been affected by similarly toxic parents and share your story. Then listen to their stories. You will find more similarities than differences. This will truly help you to understand that it was never about you. Your parents' rage, animosity, venom, whatever it was, was always about them. You are blameless. The only thing you are responsible for now is your own healing and happiness.

Releasing or limiting contact with people who have played a big role in your life is one of the hardest things you can do, and if you get to that point, you know in yourself that you are making the right decision. The good thing about hard changes like this is that you make room for new people to love, who will also love you in return. You make room for the people who will support you in your healing, instead of trying to bring you down. This does not mean that other people will not judge you for your choices, however. Some will; some won't. But whether you are judged or not, you must continue to stand your ground and know that you are making the right choices for yourself, even if other people do not understand.

Ultimately, standing up for yourself is about learning to validate yourself instead of requiring validation from other people, no matter who they are. Your romantic partner, your parents, your family members, your boss, and your co-workers have no business defining who you are, so do not let them. Only you can know who you really are, and only you can determine whether you are at peace with yourself. If you accept the judgments of others as valid, then you are giving your power away. Keep it. Let it nourish you. Let it move you. Let it bring you the peace that you deserve. Take the love that is there for you, inside of you. Find your light and let it continue to illuminate your own unique path. No one else can walk it. It is yours.

Your perfect imperfections

I used to look in the mirror and feel shame. I look in the mirror now, and I absolutely love myself.
—Drew Barrymore

We typically think of our imperfections as things we want to rid ourselves of, but take a moment to think of them as Divine Gifts.

Your imperfections are your handicap in the great game of life. If you did not have them, the game would be too easy, and what fun is that? Why bother to experience limitation and the joy of waking up again if it isn't challenging? Without your imperfections, it would be hard to convince yourself that you are less than what you really are: a divine, perfect, infinitely powerful being whose natural state is love and joy. As Robert Scheinfeld says, it is an absolute miracle that we humans have managed to convince ourselves that we are imperfect and powerless.

Your imperfections perform another useful function: they allow you to connect with others. When you recognize shared challenges and hardships, you can empathize with others. Two people with the same issues can relate. They can share, cry, laugh, struggle, and heal together. Shared human experience brings people together, and our imperfections are part of our humanity—by design.

Your Spirit is challenging you to love the things that you think do not deserve love. Everything you do not like or that makes you uncomfortable is reflecting your own imperfections back to you. This process of ceasing to judge, accepting, and ultimately loving unconditionally fires your evolution, and with each iteration in your Spirit's journey, you come closer to remembering who you are and embodying your own mastery. Without your imperfections, this would not be possible. Without your imperfections, there would not be a game of life at all.

As you give thanks for your imperfections and learn to love them, you will come upon a paradox: your imperfections do not actually exist. They are just illusions, like your ego, your perceived separation, your belief in "other." You are part of Spirit and therefore cannot be imperfect. Your imperfections are perfect; you are perfect; you are not "broken" or unworthy. All is in divine order and always has been.

Becoming comfortable with comfort

Your inner child has probably spent your entire lifetime holding onto some unhappy feelings: anger, grief, sadness, depression, anxiety, fear, or low self-esteem, to name a few. As a result, you are accustomed to living in this emotional state, and it feels normal to you. As you walk the path to your joy, however, you begin to shift and release these feelings, bit by bit. As your emotional world changes and as your consciousness changes so that you are making healthier choices for yourself, it is going to feel strange—even foreign, or just amazingly uncomfortable. When this happens, it is your inner child telling you that he or she does not feel safe with all of the changes you are making. Oh, sure, your inner child was not happy before, but at least they knew the lay of the land. But now you are changing all the rules. And that feels scary.

Making your world safe

As you learn to be comfortable with comfort, you may have to reassure your inner child often at first. Be aware that your inner child wants to revert to the old ways of doing things because he or she is afraid. Be alert to any attempts on the part of your inner child to sabotage your joy and your healing. Sometimes simply being conscious is enough to make you stop it when it happens.

On the other hand, your inner child is an emotional being, and you may find yourself feeling anxious, unsure, or even overwhelmed at times. This is perfectly natural. It is perfectly okay. When you have these feelings, give yourself the space to work through them safely.

At a time when you are not feeling anxious or upset, create a "safe space" in your home where you can go to process your feelings. It should be as quiet, private, and comfortable as possible. It could be a spot under a tree in your yard. It could be a few pillows arranged in the corner of your bedroom. It could be a warm bubble bath and a lighted candle. Whatever space you choose, decorate it in a way that makes you feel good. Make it yours.

When you are having a rough time or your inner child just needs some love and reassurance, go to this safe space and connect with your inner child. Remind them that you are moving forward to find your comfort and your joy, and that everything will be okay. Remember to reparent your inner child and tell them that you are the grown-up now, and you will keep them safe wherever you go.

Learning to trust

Trust is letting go of needing to know all the details before you open your heart.
—Author unknown

Depending on what happened to your inner child, learning to trust may sound impossible. It isn't, but it is also not something that is going to happen overnight. When practiced daily, you can learn to trust over time, but the primary goal in this must be to learn how to trust yourself and your own Spirit.

If you suffered any emotional abuse at all, you may believe that you are inherently not trustworthy because your inner child bought into all of the words and beliefs that were projected onto you by others: that you are stupid, incompetent, unworthy, or just not good enough. Your inner child may doubt your own ability to make good decisions. Your inner child may prefer to look around for authority figures to tell them what they should do. As a result, your inner child's inherent distrust has caused you to live according to what others believe instead of according to what *you* believe. If you live by other people's rules and beliefs, your joy will elude you.

To correct this, it is important that your inner child learn to trust in your own competence. Reparenting yourself and becoming your inner child's new authority figure is the first step on this path. Trust builds on itself, and when you start to trust yourself, it becomes easier the more you do it.

Begin by trusting your judgment. You are competent to discern for yourself what you need to do at any time. If your Spirit—your inner feeling—tells you that you should or should not do something, pay attention. If your inner feeling tells you that someone is or is not trustworthy, pay attention. If your inner feeling tells you that you need to make a change, pay attention. You can, of course, solicit or listen to the advice of others, but in the end, make sure that the decision is yours. Make sure that you are bought into it, and that you have not been convinced simply because the other person did a better job arguing than you did or because they have ridiculed your idea. Listen to your feelings.

As you learn to trust yourself, you can truly take your power back. You can truly own your life and your happiness. And even if others think differently or criticize your choices, you can fall back on that trust and know that you are doing what you need to do without doubting yourself. And when you can trust yourself, you can begin to trust others and let them into your world.

Exercise: Reinforcing trust in yourself

Keep a journal and start by recalling times when you did not listen to your inner feeling and did something else instead. Ask yourself some questions:

- How did that work out?
- Were you happy with the results?
- How do you feel about it now?
- Would you do it differently if you could do it again?

Next, recall the times when you *did* listen to your inner feeling, even if others disagreed with your decision. Ask yourself the same questions listed above.

For awhile, continue to record your choices and whether you listened to your inner feeling. Over time, you can see that listening to your inner feelings probably made you happier and produced better results than ignoring them. Having this information on paper will make this more real for you and your inner child.

Being seen

If you grew up in an environment in which the best way to cope was to not be seen, then you are accustomed to being invisible. For some kids, the best way to avoid the wrath or criticism of a toxic parent is to "fly under the radar" as much as possible. If you were one of those, then your challenge is to become visible again.

Visibility probably terrifies your inner child because you feel unsafe, vulnerable, and open to attack—which means that you are open to criticism and hurtful or unloving words or acts. Visibility also requires you to trust. This means trusting others when appropriate, but again, it primarily means trusting yourself and your Spirit.

Your inner child's fear of being hurt is completely rational and understandable if you were hurt or abused in any way as a child. But now that you have grown up and made the decision to find your joy, it is important to shift from being a victim of that hurt and abuse into being a powerful grown-up who is competent to navigate the world and discern for yourself.

It is certainly true that some people are just not trustworthy. Decide not to live in fear of those people. Know that you now have the power to keep these people at arm's length, and you have the ability to attract trustworthy people into your life. As you exercise your faith in yourself, this will become easier with time. Eventually, you will be able to drop the things that you have learned to use to be invisible. They may include your clothes, your weight, or the mask you wear each day when you pretend to be someone you are not.

To find your joy, you must be authentic. You must be who you really are. Some people may disapprove; maybe your parents disapprove. This is hurtful, but decide not to let that hurt rule your life. For every person who disapproves, there will be many people who love and accept you for who you really are. Give them a chance to find you. Give the people who are already in your life the chance to love that in you. In order to do that, you must let others see you. Dare to be seen.

Creating intimacy and being vulnerable

If your inner child did not experience many (or any) loving relationships or you did not have many loving relationships modeled for you, then intimacy probably does not come easily for you. Your inner child craves intimacy, but, confusingly, is terrified of it because it is the same thing as being seen. If you are truly intimate with someone, they see you. They see the real you, not your masks, not your walls, but *you*.

Intimacy is created in an environment of trust, sharing, and revealing in which the people involved can be truly authentic, honest, and vulnerable. Relationships in which this is possible are the happiest, because it fosters an environment of unconditional love and understanding.

Children naturally want to be this open and honest. In a loving environment, the parents foster intimacy within the family so that the children know that they can express themselves as they are and still be loved. On the other hand, children in less loving environments quickly discover that revealing themselves can be perilous. Being authentic can invite criticism, condemnation, or worse. In environments such as these, children learn to hide who they really are. Sometimes they do it so well that they forget who they really are.

If your inner child is afraid of revealing him- or herself, then he or she may sabotage any attempts at intimacy. But you, as the grown up, can choose to trust your partner and your children, and to let them into your world. You can build intimacy over time—but only if your partner is truly trustworthy. If you are in a relationship in which revealing yourself to your partner leaves you feeling worse than before, then you have probably chosen a partner who is familiar to your inner child—one who re-creates the old, toxic patterns of your childhood because they are familiar and therefore more comfortable than loving patterns.

Loving, trustworthy partners exist in the world for you, and as you work lovingly with your inner child and develop an intimate relationship with yourself, you will be able to develop intimate relationships with others who will not abuse the trust you place in them.

Pursuing your joy

Joy is your Spirit's natural state. Joy is available, and it is attainable. You *can* live a joy-filled life. The first step in getting there is to believe that you can. The second step is to listen to your heart and do the things that bring you joy. Take little steps. This is not a contest to win or lose. There is no right or wrong way to pursue your joy. Your joy is as unique as you are. Your purpose is as unique as you are. Let it be what it is.

When you live a joy-filled life, you are fulfilled from within. You are pursuing love, both the giving and the receiving of it. This does not mean, however, that you will never again have a bad day, or that you won't face serious challenges. But it does mean you will handle those times differently. It means you will be able to make choices that are aligned with the pursuit of your joy, even if takes awhile to achieve it or overcome certain challenges.

Joy is the choice of powerful creators. Victims, on the other hand, never choose joy. This is the only difference between these two. You are already a powerful creator. You can live that today by choosing to pursue your joy. Just ask yourself: does this choice bring me joy or heartache? Does this choice feel good, or does it cause me to feel resentful? Is this what I really want, or am I being dishonest with myself in order to please others? Is this choice helpful or unhelpful? What option (offered or not) is most appealing to me?

Pursuing your joy is about what stirs your soul and what feels authentic to you, but it is about others, too. You can pursue your joy and help others to pursue theirs at the same time. When your goal is a "win-win" for everyone, you create a greater joy than you could create alone! It is amazing how joyful you can feel when you work collectively with others to pursue joy. This is co-creation at its best, and the resulting joyful feelings grow exponentially as more people work together in this way.

As you pursue your own joy and help others pursue theirs, you will have to make trade-offs and compromises so that everyone's needs are met. At the end of the day, however, if you have made joy your goal, you will find that your life changes in miraculous ways. You may not notice at first. You may even think you are not succeeding. But remember, pursuing joy is as much a habit as pursuing misery. Your inner child learned one way of living that became ingrained over years. Be patient and allow the days, months, and years it will take to retrain your mind and body to pursue joy. Never beat yourself up for having a negative thought or feeling. You will have those, even when you pursue your joy. They are just messengers. Honor them. Let them be. Release them and just remember your goal.

If you plant a tomato seed in a garden, you will not get a tomato the next day. The seed has to germinate, and then it sprouts. Gradually, it grows taller and gets stronger and stronger. You may have to give it some support with a stake or a tomato cage. But it grows with nourishment, sunshine, and care.

Eventually it will bear fruit, and then one day you will find a ripe, red juicy tomato waiting to be savored.

Healing and finding your joy is a journey that never really ends. Enjoy the journey. It is called life. It is yours to cherish. Treat it as the divine gift it is and pursue the joy that is there for you.

Meditation: Journey into Joy

Put yourself in a quiet state and breathe deeply, inhaling through the nose, and exhaling through the mouth.

Archangel Azrael appears before you, a golden, luminous presence. She smiles and offers you her hand. Take it, and feel yourself lifted heaven-ward, leaving your body safely behind, where spirit guardians will keep watch over it for you.

From above, see yourself as Spirit sees you. You are perfect, just as you are, right now. You are loved beyond measure.

Azrael takes you higher, and eventually, you come to a beautiful cottage. A light is on inside. Azrael takes you into the cottage, where you see a fire burning in a warm, inviting fireplace. A teakettle is singing in the kitchen. On your left is a long table, set with all of your favorite foods. A place has been set for you.

As you look around, you see spirit guides and teachers standing ready to serve you. One of them comes to you and helps you into a warm, silken robe. Another leads you to the table and pours you a glass of pure ambrosia. Others serve your favorite foods on the plate in front of you. Take a moment to receive these gifts.

The spirit guides recede into the shadows, and you become aware that a man and a woman have come into the room and are standing by the fire. They call you by name and hold out their arms to you. They feel like home.

You stand up, and as you walk toward them, the man and the woman become one person—one being. As you watch, all of the spirit guides and teachers in the room step into this being as well. Golden light emanates from this being, who beckons you to join with it.

As you step into the light, you are enfolded in a warm embrace. Feel the love that all of the beings in the Universe have for you. They say to you, "You are never alone, because we are One Being. We are not separate from you and never have been."

You become aware of Archangel Raphael within the light. Gently, he shines a violet light in your heart. Feel this violet light expand and move upward to connect with your throat, third eye, crown, and upper chakras. Feel it also move downward through your chakras to below your feet. Invite your Joy to return.

The One Being shows you who you really are. Receive this vision.

The One Being reminds you how important you are. Without you, God would be incomplete. Receive this understanding.

Sit in this expanded state and receive any messages that may come.

When it is comfortable for you, allow yourself to come back to the awareness of your body and surroundings. Do whatever is comfortable for you as you return. Keep the feeling of love and joy around you.

Whenever you feel sad, unsure, or lonely, stop and remember the feeling of all these spiritual beings surrounding you and loving you. Then ask your Joy to return again.

Additional resources

It is my intention for this book to be a tool to assist you on your path to joy, but there are many other good tools out there that you should collect in your toolbox. The ones listed here are not meant to be comprehensive, but they will hopefully get you started. The world is full of wonderful people and organizations that do good work. If you need something that is not listed here, it probably exists somewhere.

In addition, you will find other materials about the inner child at my web site: www.brighthill.net

Books

The Anger Trap: Free Yourself from the Frustrations that Sabotage Your Life
by Les Carter

Toxic Parents: Overcoming Their Hurtful Legacy and Reclaiming Your Life
by Susan Forward

You Can Heal Your Life
by Louise Hay

Cards

Inner Child Cards, A Fairy-Tale Tarot
by Isha Lerner

Organizations and support groups

Adult Children of Narcissists (support group)
Web site: health.groups.yahoo.com/group/Adult-ChildrenOFNarcissits/

Alcoholics Anonymous
Web site: www.aa.org

Al-Anon/Alateen
Web site: www.al-anon.alateen.org

Borderline Personality support and information
Web sites: www.bpdfamily.com, www.bpdcentral.com

Depression and Bipolar Support Alliance
Web site: www.dbsalliance.org

Food Addicts in Recovery Anonymous
Web site: www.foodaddicts.org

Gamblers Anonymous
Web site: www.gamblersanonymous.org

Mayo Clinic (information about many conditions and mental illnesses)
Web site: www.mayoclinic.com

Narcotics Anonymous
Web site: www.na.org

National Domestic Violence Hotline
Web site: www.thehotline.org
Phone: 1.800.799.SAFE (7233)

National Institute of Mental Health (NIMH)
Web site: www.nimh.nih.gov

On-line Gamers Anonymous
Web site: www.olganon.org

Overeaters Anonymous
Web site: www.oa.org

Sex Addicts Anonymous
Web site: saa-recovery.org

Sexual Abuse:

Darkness to Light
Web site: www.darkness2light.org

Isurvive.org
Web site: www.isurvive.org

Joyful Heart Foundation
Web site: www.joyfulheartfoundation.org

Making Daughters Safe Again (for mother-daughter sexual abuse)
Web site: www.mdsa-online.org

Sibling Abuse Survivors' Information & Advocacy Network
Web site: www.sasian.org

Survivors Network of those Abused by Priests
Web site: www.snapnetwork.org

Survivors of Incest Anonymous
Web site: www.siawso.org

Toxic Parents (support group)
Web site: health.groups.yahoo.com/group/ToxicParents/

About the author

Asha Hawkesworth is a writer, speaker, and energy healer. She is the co-owner of Brighthill, a Healing Center. Her primary focus is helping people to find their joy and awaken to who they really are. In addition to this book, she and her wife, Ahnna Hawkesworth, have developed inner child workshops and other materials to help people in their healing journey. They are co-authors of *Brighthill Guided Meditations for Personal Transformation*, which is also available on CD at cdbaby.com.

Asha lives with her wife and two children in Gresham, Oregon.

www.brighthill.net

Made in the USA
Middletown, DE
08 December 2018